ART LEGACY COMPASS

Guidance for Managing, Downsizing, and
Transitioning an Artist's Studio and Estate

For Artists, Executors, Families and Advisors

ART LEGACY COMPASS

Guidance for Managing, Downsizing, and Transitioning an Artist's Studio and Estate

Mary E. Longe

My Art Dish Press

Deerfield, Illinois

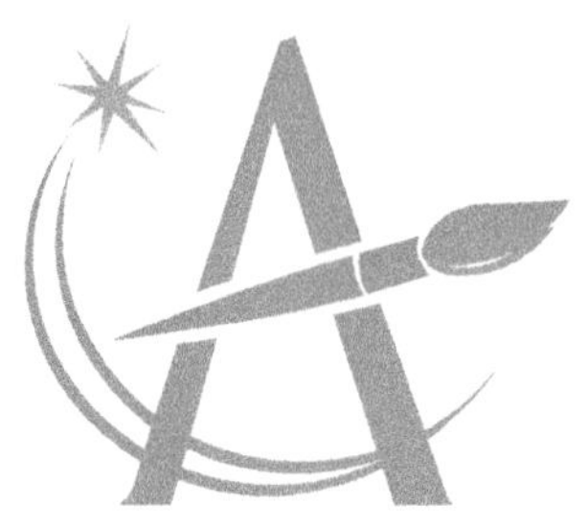

Downloadable and customizable forms referenced in the Appendix are available at www.artlegacycompass.com.

For more information, or to book an author event, please visit www.artlegacycompass.com

Publisher: My Art Dish Press

Library of Congress Control Number: 2026902903

ISBN 979-8-234-02477-0 (paperback)

ISBN 979-8-234-02478-7 (ebook)

Cover and interior design by Trinity Czarnik

Back cover photo by Claire Conley

Interior artwork by Mary Longe

Printed in the United States of America

First Edition

Legacy is not about holding on to everything.

It is about carrying forward what matters.

Art endures not only because it survives, but because it is understood, placed with care, and allowed to continue its work in the world.

When artists prepare, and when executors act with intention, art becomes more than inheritance. It becomes continuity. It becomes a living record of how one person saw—and helped shape—the world.

And that is worth securing and enduring.

For all the teachers and artists who inspired me to fill my studio—
your influence gave this book its purpose.

TABLE OF CONTENTS

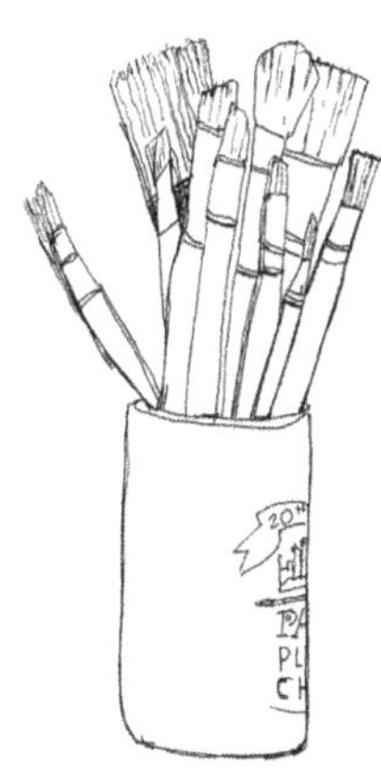

INTRODUCTION

At some point, every artist looks around the studio and realizes the question has changed.

It's no longer just *How do I make the work?* It's, *What happens to all of this?* The finished pieces. The experiments. The works-in-progress you still intend to return to. The tools that feel indispensable. The materials whose purpose is no longer obvious. The hard drive with optimistic file names. The records that quietly document a lifetime of effort.

This is not a rare moment. National data indicate that roughly 45–50% of U.S. visual artists are age 40 or older—millions in mid- to late-career stages. These figures do not fully account for crafters, teaching artists, or community-based practitioners active through ateliers, park districts, recreation programs, and local art centers. Taken together, this represents a large and growing population with decades of accumulated work, materials, records, and professional relationships.

In practical terms: a lot of studios, a lot of history, and a lot of decisions waiting to be made.

When planning has not been done in advance, heirs and executors are left to manage the volume and complexity of a working studio with little guidance. Consequential decisions are made under time pressure, emotional strain, and uncertainty about the artist's intentions.

When a Michigan painter died unexpectedly, his executor found 400 unlabeled works stacked on shelves in a damp basement. Within months, warped canvases and missing records erased provenance that could never be recovered. His children each took a few artworks. Nieces and nephews were offered others. Many went to a church rummage sale. Most went to the town dump.

The Art Legacy Compass exists to prevent that outcome.

Resources available to artists and their families are fragmented. Appraisers address value. Galleries handle sales. Estate attorneys manage legal structure. Museums serve a very small fraction of artists. Each plays an important role, but none addresses the full practical reality of a working studio. This guide brings those parts into a single, usable framework—one that helps artists, executors, and heirs make thoughtful, defensible decisions before urgency or loss forces them.

The Art Legacy Compass provides a comprehensive plan for artists and the people who will manage their work—executors, trustees, and heirs. It is for anyone who has been making art—painters, photographers, ceramicists, sculptors, quilters, doll-makers—professionals, crafters, or hobbyists with studios, craft rooms, and storage areas filled with years of trials and masterpieces, along with the equipment and supplies that created them. Over time, the steady accumulation of materials, tools, and unfinished work can quietly crowd out the physical and mental space needed to create. Thoughtful reduction prepares a studio for transition and restores room for work in the present.

Artists whose work is actively traded on the secondary market—through established resale channels or auction houses—will require more specialized, market-specific guidance. That work carries different risks, obligations, and opportunities and should be handled with advisors experienced in that marketplace. This guide then functions as a practical companion—offering structure, context, and reinforcement as decisions are made.

For everyone else, this guide helps answer a set of very human questions: What do I have? What matters most? What do I do with it? What should happen next? And how do I make those decisions in a way that respects both the work and the life behind it?

At its core, this guide is designed to help you:

- Understand what you have, without requiring perfection
- Decide what matters most, rather than treating everything as equally urgent
- Make informed, defensible decisions about sale, gift, donation, retention, or disposal
- Reduce confusion, conflict, guesswork, and burden for those who will act later

In essence, it helps you reduce what no longer serves you and open space for renewal and new work.

There is no single "right" way to reduce or disperse a studio. But there are better ways. This guide is built to help you find one that fits your circumstances and your values.

ART LEGACY COMPASS - 9 STEP GUIDANCE

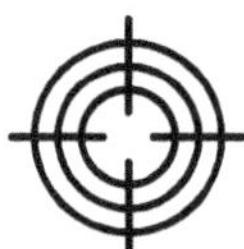

Step 1 — Clarify Your Intent and Purpose
Define why you are doing this work. Identify your priorities, constraints, and scope.

Step 2 — Identify Financial and Legal Considerations
Identify the elements that make up your art life—artwork, studio contents, records, contracts, commitments, and related materials.

Step 3 — Take Inventory
Document what exists at a level appropriate to your intent for this project. Create a usable record to support future decisions.

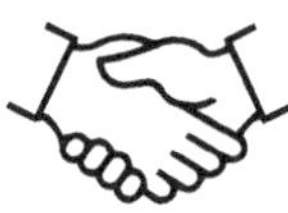

Step 4 — Establish Your Provenance
Document your legacy. This record gives future custodians the context to understand, value and exhibit your work.

Step 5 — Secure and Protect Your Art Business
Stabilize, insure, and document works appropriately. Address condition, storage, and risk before movement or disposition.

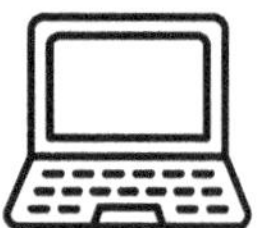

Step 6 — Document Digital Assets
Determine what digital assets exist, what they support, and what is needed to continue the business.

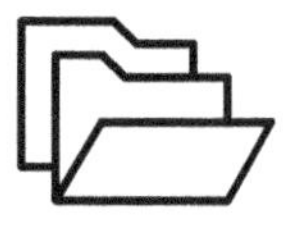

Step 7 — Downsizing & Disbursement of the Artist's Artwork & Studio
Begin the physical and administrative reduction of the studio in alignment with your decisions.

Step 8 — Prepare Instructions For Your Executor
Specify your intentions for executors, trustees, heirs, and professional advisors.

Step 9 — Complete Downsizing, & Disbursement of a Studio
Confirm that legal authority reflects your decisions and assemble the materials others will need to carry out your plan.

HOW TO USE THIS GUIDE

The section above shows where this process is headed. This section explains how to move through it.

This guide is organized into nine steps, but progress is not strictly linear. You may move back and forth between steps. For example, before building a detailed inventory in Step 3, review disposition options in Step 6 or 7. Knowing what you may ultimately do with the work should inform how much detail is necessary in documenting it.

Start with Orientation

The early steps clarify intent, constraints, and scope. Later steps provide specific pathways for disposition. Resist the urge to jump directly into sorting or documenting. Decisions made without orientation or awareness of options often create unnecessary work later.

> Despite this, most artists do not have a legacy plan or a strategy for the disposition of their studio—not because they lack concern, but because there is no clear framework for this phase of an artistic life.

Expect Nonlinear Progress

You may read ahead, revisit earlier steps, or work on multiple areas at once. Each step serves as a point of orientation, not just a box to check. Partial progress, when aligned with your overall plan, is meaningful.

Use the Artist Packet in the Appendix as your working document to record what is known, what is organized, and what is still evolving within your art estate. It allows you to shape your intentions while you are still in control.

Prepare the Executor Packet alongside it. This provides your executor with concise, practical steps to manage the business side when needed. Additional appendices offer tools and guidance for each phase of the process.

Work in Focused Sessions

This work is best done in manageable blocks of time—30 to 90 minutes. Fatigue leads to poor decisions, and poor decisions create more work later. Steady pacing is more effective than intensity.

Use the Framework, Not Perfection

You are not expected to create exhaustive documentation or resolve every uncertainty. The goal is reasonable understanding, not total certainty. In many cases, identifying what is unknown is as useful as documenting what is known. Your decisions may evolve. Revisions and course corrections are expected. This is not a one-time exercise, but an ongoing process.

Ask for Help

Inventorying and preparing artwork for disposition may require technological skills or physical effort you prefer not to handle alone. In the Appendix, you will find a sample job description for an art cataloger that can be shared with local universities offering BFA or MFA programs, or posted on community job boards to hire qualified assistance.

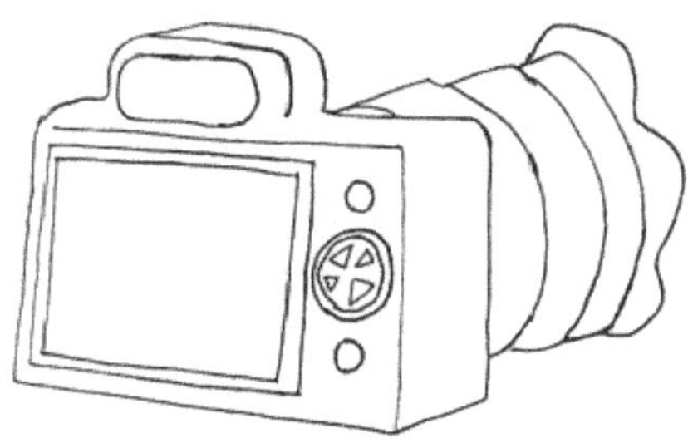

STEP 1: CLARIFY YOUR INTENT AND PURPOSE

WHY THIS STEP MATTERS

Undertaking the organization, planning, or disposition of an artist's work and studio is a substantial project. Without a clearly stated purpose, it is easy to spend time on unnecessary tasks—sorting what doesn't matter, documenting what won't be used, or getting lost in detail before you know what you are trying to accomplish.

This guide is written first and foremost for artists—those who have been working long enough to have more artwork than wall space and more bins and files than they'd like to admit. It's for artists who are still making new work, even as they begin to think about what happens to the earlier decades. Artists are best positioned to define what matters, set priorities, and provide context for their work while they are physically and mentally able to do so.

At the same time, artists rarely complete this work only for themselves. Few cleanly "wrap up" an art life. Executors, trustees, heirs, family members, and professional advisors are often the ones who must ultimately make decisions—sometimes under time pressure and without knowledge of what's what.

This guide is also written for the people and professionals who may one day be responsible for carrying out an artist's intentions.

While each reader approaches this guide from a different position, the shared need is the same: clarity, direction, and enough structure to make thoughtful decisions without having to reconstruct the artist's intent from scratch.

This first step clarifies why you are doing this work now and helps determine what needs to be done, how much detail is appropriate, and where to begin. Your process may evolve, but starting with a stated purpose keeps each subsequent step aligned. As you move through the guide, this step remains your compass—the point you return to when choices multiply or energy dips.

This step also marks the moment when private reflection begins to translate into usable guidance. You are not expected to have complete answers or final legal instructions. Articulating priorities and context reduces the likelihood that someone else will have to interpret your life's work under pressure.

The materials you create beginning here—notes, worksheets, early guidance—should be kept together in a dedicated folder (digital, physical, or both) and stored alongside your estate planning documents. Even if you pause midway, what you record now still carries value.

WHAT TO DO

Review the following reasons artists begin to organize their art business and studios. Take time to consider these or others that reflect your art life and current situation and goals.

Studio Organization and Personal Readiness
- Spring cleaning and basic organization of artwork, materials, tools, and records
- Downsizing in anticipation of a move, space reduction, health change, or transition to new medium, technique or art

- Gaining a clear understanding of what exists, where it is, and what matters most

Planning for Artwork, Archives, and Legacy

- Preparing artwork, archives, and materials for future sale, donation, gifting, or responsible disposal
- Clarifying which works or materials hold cultural, financial, or institutional significance
- Preparing work for curatorial review, exhibition, archival placement, or institutional donation
- Creating structure so galleries, advisors, or appraisers can understand the scope and history of the work

Legal, Financial, and Administrative Preparation

- Establishing documentation to support estate planning, probate, or trust administration
- Supporting legal planning, valuation, or tax-related decision-making
- Organizing information for financial planners to evaluate assets and income streams
- Preparing guidance for attorneys, trustees, or professional executors

Transition and Capacity Planning

- Preparing for relocation or assisted living by identifying what must move, be stored, or be resolved
- Documenting priorities so decisions can be made responsibly during periods of stress or limited capacity

Executor and Heir Support

- Reducing uncertainty and decision-making burden
- Establishing a roadmap so multiple professionals can work in parallel without duplicating effort

FURTHER DEFINE YOUR INTENDED OUTCOMES

Describe your role and the outcome you want to achieve.

Example for Artists

By the end of this project, I want my artwork and studio organized enough that I understand what I have, where it is, and what matters most. I want key decisions made—about what should be preserved, sold, donated, or released—so they are not deferred or left ambiguous. I want it to be easier for someone else to step in without misinterpreting my intentions.

Example for Executors

By the end of this project, I want a clear understanding of the artist's work, studio, and professional relationships so I am not forced to guess. I want materials labeled, records consolidated, and priorities identified so I can act responsibly and confidently.

Example for Art, Legal, Financial, and Social Work Professionals

By the end of this project, I want artwork, documentation, and priorities identified so I am not reconstructing context or filling gaps. I want to provide appropriate guidance efficiently and without misalignment.

TIMELINE PROMPT

Now describe your intended time horizon:

- Immediate (weeks)

- Short-term (6–12 months)

- Long-term (multi-year)

Note any circumstances that may influence this timeline (health, space constraints, relocation, estate planning milestones).

FINANCIAL INTENT

When clarifying your overall intent, it's also essential to define your financial intent. Are you working to grow the financial value of your art business—through sales, licensing, or commissions? Or is your priority thoughtful placement, whether through gifts, donations, or selective transfers to people and institutions you value? Stating this clearly gives you a practical framework for decisions you are making now—about pricing, production, representation, retention, and distribution.

For example, you might write:

My priority is to maximize the financial value of my art business and estate, strengthening its market position over time.

Or:

My priority is thoughtful placement of my work, balancing financial return with meaningful distribution to collectors, family, and institutions.

Written plainly, this kind of statement becomes a working directive—guiding choices today as well as in any future transition.

> Art Legacy Compass is also designed for: Legal, financial, real estate, health, and community professionals commonly involved in artist transitions and estates—appraisers, advisors, gallerists, conservators, art handlers, attorneys, trust and estate administrators, financial planners, senior move managers, estate clean-out professionals, social workers, and others whose work depends on clear information and well-articulated priorities.

A COMMON PITFALL TO AVOID — ASSUMING THIS PROJECT IS ONLY ABOUT OBJECTS

Decisions about artwork and studios are not just about objects. They are shaped by emotion, memory, identity, and responsibility.

One seventy-year-old painter with work in museums and galleries, was surprised by how emotionally draining his studio clean-out became. He eventually recognized he was grieving—not only for the works he was releasing, but for the period of life they represented. Once he named that grief, the work became easier. He kept only a handful of meaningful pieces. When the nearly five-month process ended, he felt renewed energy and returned to making work with focus and momentum.

There is no shortage of television shows, books, podcasts, and social media devoted to organizing, tidying, and decluttering. Everywhere you look, someone is promising a cleaner closet, a calmer kitchen, or a lighter life.

On TikTok and Instagram, Baby Boomers are often shamed for "generational guilt" passed on to their Millennial and Gen X kids—guilt they inherited themselves. But when you talk with Boomers, it's more practical: their kids just don't want the china, oak dining sets, figurines, or model airplanes. It's not rejection—just a shift in lifestyle, space, and priorities. Boomers and the generation before are left wondering what to do with it all.

In families of artists, the dynamic is only slightly different.

An idea to lift some of the emotional burden of this project: Gather 20 photographs of your favorite artworks from across your career. Use an online service to turn those images into a photobook— a snapshot of your artistic journey.

Heirs may value the artwork deeply. They may choose—sometimes even argue over—a handful of meaningful pieces. But they don't want the remaining 185 works.

And that's where the real complexity begins.

Beyond the logistics lies something much more tender: the guilt and sadness of letting go of something a parent, grandparent, aunt, or uncle created with care and intention.

For heirs, these decisions are not about taste or square footage alone. They are about love, memory, and the quiet fear of dishonoring a life's work.

Whether you are the artist or the heir, this process involves both gratitude and grief. Recognizing that truth makes clearer decisions possible.

YOUR GUIDANCE FOR YOUR EXECUTOR, TRUSTEE, OR HEIRS

After clarifying your overall intent, declaring your financial intent, and the time horizon, begin recording what you already understand about your art estate in a form someone else could follow. You will find a worksheet, the **ART ESTATE NAVIGATOR** in the Appendix for this purpose. This is not yet about final legal language. It is about capturing a clear snapshot of your current understanding—your studio, your artwork, your priorities.

As you move through later Steps, this guidance becomes more specific. But its value begins now. Even partial clarity reduces guesswork.

WHEN TO USE AN ATTORNEY IN PLANNING OR AS EXECUTOR

Even modest estates may include tasks that require professional legal guidance. Legal, other professional fees, or executor compensation can be paid by the estate. Noting this in executor instructions may reduce hesitation about taking on the role.

Artists typically collect art. Use this process to collect the information you need to make decisions about the disposition of your own artwork and your "owned art."

If your art estate includes sizable assets, you will need an attorney to structure your will or trust properly. Thorough record keeping is essential. Estate funds may cover expenses such as a sale, but all expenditures must be documented and accounted for.

The structure of the artist's business determines additional responsibilities. If the business has its own EIN and separate tax filings, a final return must be filed under that EIN. If income has been reported under a Social Security number, the executor should apply for a new EIN to wind up the business. The appropriate approach depends on scale and complexity—another reason professional guidance is often necessary. You will find in the **APPENDIX – MEETING WITH ATTORNEY - DISCUSSION GUIDE,** a checklist to prepare for an efficient and focused conversation with an attorney.

Formal executor instructions, legal alignment, and administrative timelines are addressed more fully in Step 8, with a detailed checklist in the Appendix.

WORKSHEETS TO BEGIN NOW

Several Appendix tools support you throughout this project:

APPENDIX | STEP 1 — ART ESTATE NAVIGATOR

Begin this worksheet now and refine it as you progress in organizing or closing your art practice. It serves as your working record of what is known, what is organized, and what is still evolving within your art estate.

APPENDIX | STEP 1 — CHECKLIST FOR MY EXECUTOR — THE FIRST 90 DAYS

This worksheet functions as a practical companion for an executor-identifying the immediate tasks that must be addressed following an artist's death. It helps executors prioritize early action and helps artists see what information will matter most.

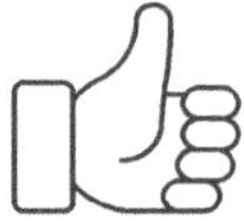

GOOD ENOUGH GUIDANCE

This step does not require final answers. It requires commitment to a direction. Even a rough statement of purpose is enough to move forward and can be refined over time.

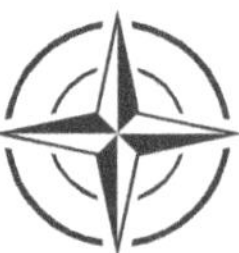

COMPASS CHECK-IN

If you could accomplish only one thing through this entire process, what would matter most—to you, or to those who will inherit responsibility for this work?

REMINDER: ART ESTATE NAVIGATOR

In the next 72 hours, complete Section 1 (one page) of the **ART ESTATE NAVIGATOR.** This 10–minute task establishes key information about your art estate. You are welcome to download that worksheet at www.artlegacycompass.com, or use the outline in the Appendix to create your own. Also, add a 15-minute calendar appointment to complete Sections 2 and 3 this week.

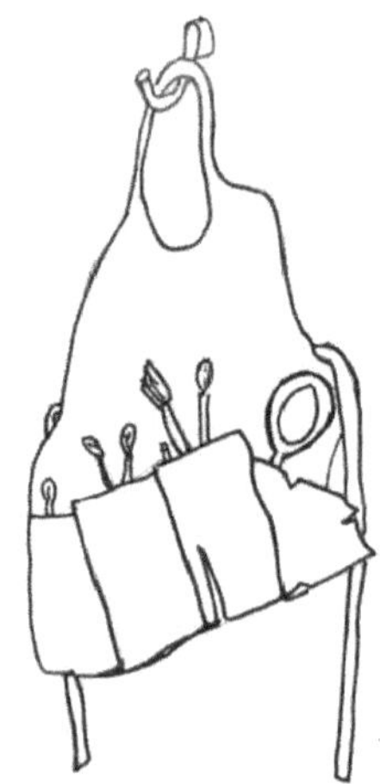

STEP 2: IDENTIFY FINANCIAL AND LEGAL CONSIDERATIONS

WHY THIS STEP MATTERS

While art making may be your raison d'être, sustaining a practice for some artists depends on the business structures that support it. Most artists rely on a combination of income streams—some steady, some intermittent, and some tied to specific works, platforms, or professional relationships. As an artist adds income streams, or contracts are signed with galleries or loans of artwork are made to a municipality, guidance from a financial or legal expert is prudent.

Whether you are closing or downsizing your practice, use this as your **Alignment Moment**—a deliberate pause before taking on the other Steps in this project. As a working artist, use it as a checkpoint. Are your current efforts aligned with what you say you want? Is your pricing consistent with growth? Are you building the relationships that support thoughtful placement? Legacy is not formed at the end of a career—this moment of reflection is your opportunity to strengthen your practice while you are still building it.

In considering estate planning, documenting how income flows through a practice clarifies what generates revenue and provides essential guidance for heirs, executors, and advisors who may need to manage, conclude, or transfer these arrangements. Documenting the processes, people and places that are involved in the artist's finances is critical for all concerned.

ONE ARTIST'S EXPERIENCE

A painter in Portland, Oregon, earns his living from many sources. He sells from his easel while painting plein air and often wins prize money in juried competitions, each with an entry fee. He shows and sells through a local artist group sponsored by a community art center and is represented by galleries in Wisconsin and Oregon. These sales generate commission splits and annual 1099 tax forms. Because of his reputation, he is rarely without a commissioned painting—often a portrait of a home or beloved pet—and there is usually a waiting list. A couple of times each year, he also teaches an online course for an art center.

His income depends on many moving parts. For clarity in administering the estate, each source should be listed in the **ART ESTATE NAVIGATOR** in the Appendix, so that contracts, payment records, and tax reporting streams are not overlooked. Those 1099 forms, in particular, help an executor identify income sources, reconcile payments, and ensure final tax filings are accurate.

If he were gone tomorrow, the commissioned works in progress and his gallery relationships would require immediate attention due to contracts, delivery commitments, and pending payments. As a courtesy, the competitions, artist group, and art center should also be notified—but the active commissions, galleries come first.

WHAT TO DO
Business Structure
We assume you have figured out your business structure, whether a

sole proprietorship, or a type of corporation. This should be made clear to your executor to make future decisions. Of course, if your business structure is complicated, an attorney, and/or an accountant should give guidance.

Bank Accounts

Executors may need to open an estate bank account; to do so, they will need an appropriate EIN from the IRS. You can't just open a bank account without it. If there is a trust - you must obtain the EIN for the trust, and the bank account is opened in the name of the trust and that EIN is used. If no trust, a probate estate must be opened before you can open an estate bank account. This is hugely difficult without guidance from an attorney.

Income Streams

Create a list of all current and recent art-related income streams. Provide the information that someone else will need to access and make sense of them. Use a spreadsheet or complete the **APPENDIX – ART ESTATE NAVIGATOR** to document this element of your art business practice.

For each income stream, note:

- Status (active / occasional / discontinued)
- Any ongoing commitments or upcoming obligations
- Location of related contracts, invoices, correspondence, or files
- Whether the income source generates tax forms (e.g., 1099s)
- Key contacts, including names, roles, organizations, and departments
- Passwords
- For online platforms: how income is generated and where login credentials are stored

The goal is to make existing arrangements visible and understandable to someone else.

Common Art-Related Income Streams

Use this list as a starting point. Add others as needed.

- Art sales (original works, editions, prints, digital works)
- Where sales typically occur, pricing practices, and any gallery or commission agreements.
- Teaching / workshops (in-person or online)
- Scheduled commitments, institutional affiliations, and who should be notified if changes are required.
- Consulting / advising
- Scope and duration of engagements, and whether relationships are ongoing or project based.
- Licensing / royalties / sponsorships
- Contract terms, duration, renewal or expiration conditions, and how payments are received.
- Loans of artwork
- Locations, duration, insurance requirements, and return procedures.
- Other: ____
- Grants, stipends, residencies, or cooperative revenue arrangements.

FINANCIAL RECORDS

An executor will need a clear picture of the financial side of your art practice. This includes recent tax returns, 1099 forms, sales records, commission agreements, gallery contracts, licensing agreements, bank accounts related to the business, insurance policies, and documentation of any outstanding payments or receivables. Digital sales platforms, online payment processors, and subscription services should also be identified. Take time now to gather these records and, just as importantly, note where they are located—whether in a file cabinet, a cloud drive, an accountant's office, or within specific online accounts. A note in the **ART ESTATE NAVIGATOR** or a simple summary sheet pointing to these sources can save significant time, expense, and confusion later.

YOUR PRICING STRATEGY

Because galleries operate as businesses, they evaluate artists through the lens of market viability. Most set informal pricing thresholds, and until an artist's

> Your pricing should evolve with your career. Adjust your prices when you add meaningful credentials—awards, exhibitions, press recognition, or institutional placements. Thus, pricing growth supports your professional standing and reassures collectors that your work holds its value.

work consistently sells within those ranges, representation is unlikely. Gallery pricing typically reflects commission structures—often around fifty percent of the retail price—which means the final price is set high enough to support both the artist and the gallery. Once work is priced at gallery levels, that pricing becomes the market reference point; all other sales channels should align accordingly to maintain consistency and protect collector confidence.

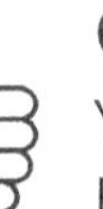

GOOD ENOUGH GUIDANCE

You do not need perfect financial records to complete this step. Even partial information—platform names, types of income, or general descriptions—can significantly reduce confusion later. This step is about visibility, not accounting precision. (Though that helps in the long run.)

COMPASS CHECK-IN

Which income streams would be most difficult for someone else to identify or responsibly manage without your input? Leaving good notes or orienting your executor to your financial systems will make this transition much easier.

REMINDER: ART ESTATE NAVIGATOR

Take a moment to update any sections of the **ART ESTATE NAVIGATOR** that are clearer now. Even brief notes help reduce uncertainty later and will be incorporated into more detailed instructions in later steps.

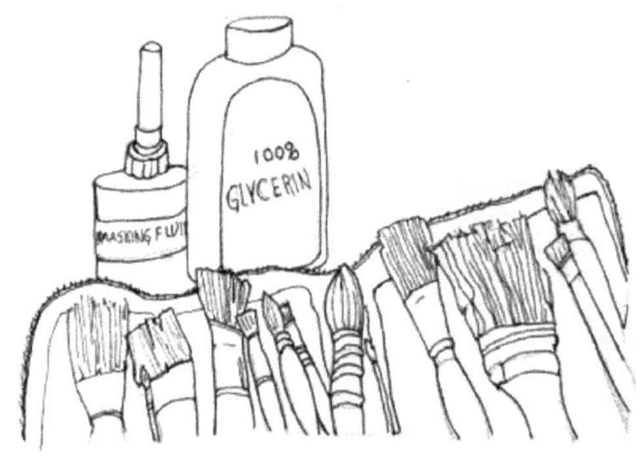

STEP 3: TAKE INVENTORY

WHY THIS STEP MATTERS

For many artists, the visible accumulation of artwork, tools, and materials is what finally prompts the need to pause and take stock. In Step 1, you clarified your objectives and financial direction. In Step 2, you identified the legal and structural elements that shape your art estate—contracts, commitments, and income streams. Now, you turn to the tangible: the artwork, materials, and equipment that have accumulated over time, so you can see the full scope of what exists. An accurate inventory makes every later decision easier, whether you are organizing, downsizing, preparing for disposition, or supporting heirs or an executor. (See **STEP 4: ESTABLISH YOUR PROVENANCE** for guidance on documenting the information that helps protect the value of your work.)

Remember why you are undertaking this project. Be ruthless and take a hard, honest look at your studio—and by "studio," we mean every place your work happens or lives: a professional studio, co-op space, spare bedroom, garage, basement, attic, storage unit, digital archive, or off-site facility—anywhere you create, assemble, store, or stage your work. Anything that is broken or unsafe should be discarded immediately. If something is unlikely ever to be finished don't inventory it.

Inventory is not busywork. It is direction. When you document quantities, add images, record dimensions, note condition, and match works to their locations or sales, you begin to see the full scope of your practice. The numbers reveal scale. The photographs reconnect you with the work. Condition notes protect value. Matching works to collectors or storage prevents confusion later.

Just as importantly, inventorying requires you to look closely. You may recognize patterns, rediscover strengths, or see unfinished ideas with a new perspective. You gain a realistic sense of what you have created—and, over time, a clearer understanding of the financial value of your holdings.

That information is the foundation for action. It informs pricing, exhibitions, insurance, storage, and placement decisions. It also provides an executor with a practical starting point for valuation—what exists, what has sold, what may be marketable, and what requires professional appraisal. Instead of guessing, they have a structured framework from which to proceed.

PREPARE TO INVENTORY

Inventory Tools and Systems

Use a spreadsheet, word-processing document, or art inventory software. Format matters less than consistency and accessibility.

When choosing an art inventory system for managing a visual arts collection, start with how you work, not with software features. The system should make it easy to create clear records for each artwork, upload high-quality images, and add notes about condition, location, value and provenance - the documented history or ownership. Look for flexible fields so you can track what matters most to you, whether that is exhibitions, sales history, or insurance details.

The right system should also be able to grow with your collection over time. Some platforms allow you to connect your inventory to a

> **Legacy First, Inventory Second.**
>
> Before you start counting, measuring, and labeling, take a moment to think about what you want your work to say to the generations that come next. Your notes about the artwork can make a difference. Inventory records what exists; legacy clarifies what matters.

website, client contact list, or accounting records, which can be helpful but is not required at the beginning. Cloud-based access is important so you or someone assisting you can securely view and update records from anywhere. Before deciding, check that training materials or customer support are available, and compare pricing and user reviews. Choose a system that feels manageable, fits your budget, and supports your long-term goals rather than one that feels overly complex or intimidating.

An Excel worksheet or Google Sheets may work well for smaller holdings. However, after inventorying a collection of 5,000 works—and hearing similar experiences from other artists—Art Legacy Compass recommends using a dedicated art inventory platform, www.ArtworkArchive.com. These systems are designed specifically for artists and collectors, are relatively intuitive to use, and include features that support both day-to-day studio management and long-term estate planning and management.

Inventory Guidelines

STEP 7: DOWNSIZING & DISPOSITION OF THE ARTIST'S ARTWORK AND STUDIO sparks ideas for places where you might let works go to - do not spend time cataloging objects that carry no realistic future use or value for you or others.

Prepare and call ahead to donate piles of art magazines, bins of materials from abandoned projects or past crafts that, likely, will never be revisited. Make it a practice when you are out and about your community, to query which local arts and craft stores, art centers, senior centers, park districts take donations of art and art supplies.

A clerk at a nearby knit shop mentioned that they are happy to take yarns, patterns, needles, unfinished projects, because they use them to teach refugees to knit, make blankets for veterans, babies and cancer patients, and respond to requests from senior centers.

Be ruthless. Remove what is not salvageable so the inventory reflects only what truly remains in play. If tracking items individually would not change how they are stored, valued, sold, donated, or disposed of, they do not require individual inventory records.

Not every artist's situation requires the same depth of documentation. Artists with established markets or higher-value works benefit from detailed, item-level records.

In some cases, a high-level description is sufficient—for example, noting "20 blue 10-inch vases, assorted glazes"—when individual records would add little meaningful value.

NOTE TO EXECUTORS

Executors are not expected to preserve everything in an artist's studio. Letting go of materials, unfinished works, and surplus items is not a failure of stewardship. It is often a necessary and responsible part of the process. The goal is not total preservation, but informed decision-making that reflects the artist's wishes, their standing, intent, and realistic future use of the work.

INVENTORYING ARTWORK

For each piece, include:

Accession Number

Depending on the situation, you may assign a unique accession number—a tracking number recorded in your inventory—to identify and monitor the artwork. Some artists choose to discreetly mark this number on the artwork itself—typically on the back or underside with a marker or sticker—while others rely solely on documentation.

Title / Identifier

Distinguishes one work from another and prevents confusion among similar or related pieces, prints, etc. This becomes the primary reference point for tracking, discussion, and decisions. "Untitled 1, 2, or 3" isn't provocative—it's just uncreative. (IMHO)

Artist Name (or Artist of Owned Art)

Establishes authorship and ownership context. This is essential for copyright, valuation, and decision-making authority.

Medium / Type

Identifies materials and format, which affects value, handling, storage, and conservation needs. It also signals which professionals may be required.

Dimensions

Critical for storage, shipping, insurance, exhibition, and resale. Size often directly affects cost and feasibility of disposition.

Date / Year Created

Places the work within the artist's career timeline. This can influence historical significance, market interest, and valuation.

Price

Supplies a factual market reference. Even if outdated, it helps guide future pricing and expectations.

Valuation (if known)

Provides a starting point for insurance, estate accounting, or distribution, especially for owned art. Noting the source of the valuation helps assess reliability. Resources for valuation are described below.

Notes Supporting Value (exhibitions, awards, provenance)

Records professional context that may not be evident from the work alone. These details can materially affect cultural and financial value. Step 4 provides detail.

Location

Current Location, including if it is on loan or exhibited. Ensures the work can be located quickly and accurately. This is essential when work is stored in multiple rooms, facilities, off-site or on loan. If the art estate is large, items are spread out, it may be helpful to assign a location code as broadly as a room name, or specifically to an individual storage area, i.e., shelf, rack, box, drawer. Minimal handling, easy access and overall efficiency drive this.

Condition

The condition of a piece of art directly affects value, insurability, and next steps, which is particularly important in insurance considerations. Condition reports document the physical state of artwork and establish a baseline record. Include written descriptions, additional photographs noting surface condition, existing damage, framing, and mounting. Condition reports should be completed before and after loans, exhibitions, shipping, storage transfers, sales, or donations. Maintaining these records protects the estate by clarifying responsibility and supporting insurance claims if damage occurs.

Status (sold / available / on loan / in progress / needs repair)

Clarifies what actions are appropriate or restricted. This prevents errors such as unauthorized sales or premature disposal.

Disposition Instructions (by Artist for Executor/Heir)

Translates intent into actionable guidance. Clear instructions reduce guesswork and conflict later. Step 8 provides detail.

Series

Describes how the artist has used or refers to groupings of work, including themes, exhibits, media. Later, these potentially can be grouped for future shows or other uses.

Photos (front / back / details)

Provides visual identification and condition reference. Photos are essential for insurance, appraisal, and remote review. Disposition may be dependent on photos. Good lighting and clear focus are crucial.

INVENTORY PROFESSIONAL CONTACTS

Most archival systems include contacts. It will be helpful to whomever is responsible for the next steps of your art estate to have the contacts easily accessible. Use your inventory system as a central source for galleries, framers, foundries, agents, printers, conservators, storage facilities, and press contacts. If you aren't using an app or system, use your phone to categorize your professional contacts. Put the word Studio as their middle name or business name, followed by a dash and their role, for example, Studio-Framer, -Art Supply, -Instructor.

ONE ARTIST'S EXPERIENCE

A Chicago artist has used a professional artwork management system for more than ten years. It took time to upload earlier pieces, but today every sold and available work is documented in one organized database. He links his website directly to the system rather than juggling multiple platforms, creates tailored viewing rooms when approaching new galleries, and can download sales reports and collector information whenever he needs them for taxes or outreach.

What began as a simple inventory tool has become the backbone of his art business.

More importantly, if he ever decides to downsize his studio, step back from exhibitions, or close his practice altogether, he already knows what he has documented, what has sold, who owns what, and how to reach the people connected to his work. That certainty turns what could be an overwhelming process into a manageable one.

PROFESSIONAL ASSISTANCE:

Artwork Cataloger – If you are at a point in needing help to inventory your personal and/or owned artwork, a position description for an artwork cataloger can be found in the Appendix. Personalize it, send it around to friends, post it on digital and actual job boards at universities with BFA or MFA programs.

MAINTAINING THE INTEGRITY OF ARTWORK AS IT LEAVES THE STUDIO

Once an artwork can be reliably identified within an inventory, the next consideration is how that identification supports long-term tracking, verification, and protection as work moves beyond the studio.

Protecting the integrity of the artwork is one of the main reasons inventory matters. For the artist, good records protect authorship and intent, ensuring that work in circulation is properly attributed and accurately described. For executors and heirs, that documentation helps prevent loss, confusion, or substitution—especially when work is loaned, consigned, or moved. A reliable inventory confirms that the piece returned is the original, not a misidentified or incorrect work. Images, identifiers, and records are not about suspicion; they ensure continuity as the work passes through different hands.

Emerging technologies—such as digital registries, blockchain records, or NFTs—are sometimes used to support this tracking. When created by the artist and tied to accurate documentation, these tools can provide time-stamped records and a visible chain of custody that strengthens provenance. However, they do not authenticate artwork on their own and should be understood as supplements to, not replacements for, a well-maintained inventory. Their value lies in reinforcing clarity: connecting a physical work to its documentation, supporting transfer records, and reducing ambiguity when artwork moves through galleries, estates, or secondary markets.

In parts of Europe, resale royalty rights recognize that artists should share in the success of their work when it is resold, granting them a percentage of future sales. This system depends on the ability to identify and trace artwork accurately as it changes hands—recognizing that creative labor continues to have value beyond the first sale. While this framework is not yet widely established in the United States, the underlying philosophy is gaining traction: that artists' interests do not end at the studio door, and that responsible tracking supports fairness, transparency, and long-term stewardship. Whether or not resale royalties apply, inventorying with an eye toward future movement affirms that artwork is not static property, but an enduring cultural and economic asset whose integrity deserves protection.

RESOURCES FOR THE VALUATION OF ARTWORK

Artists will have set prices for their work, establishing what the market has paid for it. Posthumously, unless the artist was widely known, it is unlikely that value or price will increase. Executors and heirs should generally use the artist's established pricing.

If you need assistance, especially with owned art, contact a Certified Art Appraiser to provide independent, documented opinion of value for artwork and related objects. Their work supports estate planning, probate, insurance, charitable donation, and tax reporting. Appraisers analyze condition, provenance, market history, and comparable sales to establish value for a specific purpose. Appraisers often specialize. In the best of worlds, find one that knows the genre of artwork you are valuing.

PROFESSIONAL ASSISTANCE:

Appraisers – Appraisers do not sell artwork and do not benefit from sales outcomes. Their role is neutral and analytical, and work on a fee-for-service basis.

A certified art appraiser is qualified through a combination of formal education, specialized training, professional affiliation, and adherence to ethical standards. Most have academic backgrounds in art history, fine arts, museum studies, or related fields, often supplemented by years of hands-on experience working with galleries, auction houses, museums, or private collections. Certification typically comes through recognized professional organizations such as the Appraisers Association of America, the International Society of Appraisers, or the American Society of Appraisers, each of which requires rigorous coursework, examinations, peer review, continuing education, and compliance with the Uniform Standards of Professional Appraisal Practice (USPAP). Beyond credentials, a qualified appraiser demonstrates subject-matter expertise in specific categories of art and maintains independence, objectivity, and market awareness—qualities essential for credible valuations used in estate planning, insurance, donations, or tax reporting.

INVENTORYING SUPPLIES, EQUIPMENT AND FURNITURE

Studio contents beyond artwork include:

- **Supplies:** consumables (paints, solvents, clay, sealants, yarns, inks, adhesives, glazes, fixatives, canvases, panels, paper, stretcher bars, framing materials)

- **Equipment:** reusable tools and machines (presses, kilns, wheels, sewing machines, looms, cameras, lighting equipment, computers, printers, projectors, cutting tools, power tools)

- **Furniture:** easels, tables, drafting stations, racks, flat files, shelving, storage cabinets, pedestals, display panels

- **Books and Reference Materials:** artist monographs, exhibition catalogs, technical/how-to manuals

- **Sketchbooks and Development Materials:** sketchbooks, maquettes, prototypes, studies, test prints, reference binders

- **Archives and Records:** correspondence, contracts, sales records, loan agreements, inventory lists, condition reports, receipts, tax documentation, business licenses

- **Recognition and Career Materials:** awards, certificates, exhibition posters, catalogs, press clippings, programs, artist statements, resumes, promotional materials

- **Personal and Process Materials:** journals, studio notes, idea files, research folders, digital files and hard drives, labeled file boxes

- **Framing and Packing Materials:** crates, glass, frames, mat boards, backing boards, hardware, packing supplies

Items such as these, may be listed and valued for disposition, but don't need to be inventoried. Furniture and some large or expensive equipment could be included in an inventory system as an estate is being dissolved. In that case, photos and dimensions should be taken, and a more detailed description of each item. If there's any history to an easel, for example, add a note, it will make it more endearing to the next user.

Mystery Tools & Equipment

Use Google Images or an app like Curio, to determine the use of unrecognizable equipment or supplies, and if some items have vintage value. A tube roller/paint tube wringer, brayer, palette knife or odd rubber spatulas, mahl sticks, modeling tools, silk screen squeegee, drying racks, kiln shelves, are all essential to artists at various times, but less likely to be part of the average person's awareness or lexicon. Someone will appreciate them, so don't discard items without some exploration.

Consumable supplies are most likely to be disposed of through donations or estate sales. There's no great value in documenting every tube of paint or can of solvents. However, if the artist has certain items, such as high value sable brushes it will be helpful to note that and perhaps keep them separate.

For each of these items, use as many of the same headings as for artwork, but it may be useful to include:

- Description
- Material
- Manufacturer
- Quantity
- Condition
- Estimated value
- Notes

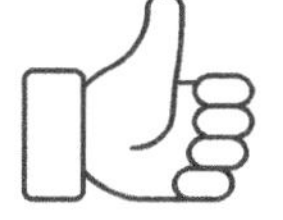

GOOD ENOUGH GUIDANCE

An inventory does not need to be complete to be useful. Even a partial record reduces future burden and guesswork, providing clarity when it matters most. Having a general sense—early in the process—of where most items might ultimately go, or quickly go, can significantly ease decision-making and emotional strain. With that orientation in place, time can then be taken to research options more carefully and identify dispositions that offer the best outcomes for the work and for the estate.

COMPASS CHECK-IN

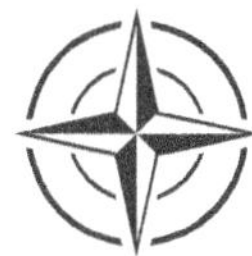

What did you discover that changes how you think about the scope or priorities of this project? Given the apparent scope of your art practice, how will you inventory your studio?

REMINDER: ART ESTATE NAVIGATOR

Realistically, taking inventory may take time depending on the size and scope of the studio. Any progress on this step will move your entire project forward.

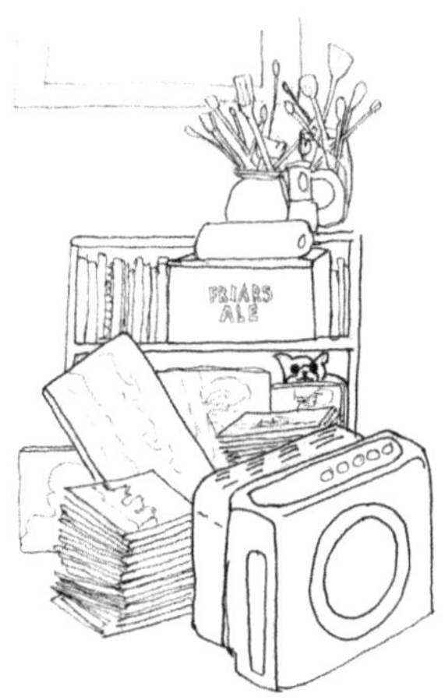

STEP 4: ESTABLISH YOUR PROVENANCE

WHY THIS STEP MATTERS

Provenance is documented legacy. It's the record of a work of art—where it has lived, how it has been shown, and the story it has carried over time. That record gives future custodians the context they need to understand, value, exhibit, sell, or responsibly place the work. And it isn't just for museum-bound artists; it matters for anyone whose work may outlast the studio in which it was made.

Establishing provenance isn't about inflating importance or rewriting history. It's about documenting what exists so others—galleries, donors, heirs, executors, and scholars—don't have to rely on memory or guesswork. It applies to work you've created as well as work you own or manage.

Most inventory systems or worksheets discussed in Step 3, allow space for provenance details, and those records may eventually be viewed by galleries, buyers, or researchers. Heirs and family members will appreciate this information just as much—clear records make it far easier to care for, place, or make decisions about the work in the future.

WHAT PROVENANCE INCLUDES

This step focuses on creating a complete internal record, regardless of what is shared publicly.

For your own artwork, provenance also includes clear identification. Your name should be associated with every piece. A front-facing signature is not required, but your name and basic identifying information should be accessible on the back or through attached documentation. For sculptures and three-dimensional works, discrete labels, tags, or QR codes may be useful.

> Buyers love the inside story.
>
> When collectors understand the context, backstory, or exhibition history behind a piece, it deepens their connection to the work—and strengthens their confidence in acquiring it. Provide a bio and thank you note when delivering your artwork.

A provenance narrative may include:

- Exhibitions
- Galleries or dealers
- Museum or institutional involvement
- Consignments and loans
- Publications or press
- Awards, grants, or residencies
- Education or mentorship
- Artist or project statements

What to Do

Using items in the inventory created in Step 3, or while you are in the process of taking inventory, assemble provenance materials at two levels:

- Artist Documentation
- Work- or series-specific documentation

- Financial Context
- Gallery and Consignment Documentation

Artist Documentation: Gather biographies, artist statements, CVs, education history, awards, grants, residencies, critiques, and press coverage. Maintain a complete master record, along with separate public-facing versions when appropriate. Promotional materials such as exhibition ads or posters that identify the artist may also be included.

While you are at it, gather and enter the names of current contacts for your organizational relationships, and for those who have collected/purchased your art. Collectors are a reflection of the artist. For some artists, high-profile collectors may increase the value of the art. This information is not shared publicly.

Work- or Series-Specific Documentation: Gather exhibition histories, catalog texts, press mentions, awards, and notes on loans or ownership for individual works or series. Link all supporting materials directly to inventory entries. Like the story about the Monet painting, the wall title cards are useful too.

In a January 28, 2025, Instagram post, a conservator from the Brooklyn Museum shows the back of Monet's *Houses of Parliament* painting covered with the wall tags from decades of previous exhibits; they referred to it as its passport.

Financial Context - Pricing History & Sales Records (Provenance Context):

Dates, pricing and sales records form an essential part of an artwork's provenance. They show how a work has been positioned and valued over time, providing factual continuity for future decisions about appraisal, sale, donation, or insurance. For an executor, these records replace reconstruction and guesswork with evidence. For appraisers, galleries, and buyers, they establish credibility and market context rather than a single fixed value.

Documenting pricing history does not mean freezing a work's worth or justifying past decisions. Prices change with markets, venues, and timing. What matters is preserving an accurate record of what was asked, what was paid, and under what circumstances. This includes gallery retail prices, direct-sale prices, discounts, commissions, and formal appraisals. When these records are scattered, missing, or informal, executors are often forced to reconstruct history under pressure—sometimes years later—leading to delays, undervaluation, or inconsistent outcomes.

Clear documentation allows future handlers of the work to identify patterns, understand prior market placement, and respond confidently to questions about value. It also protects the artist's legacy by demonstrating that pricing decisions were deliberate and grounded in actual transactions rather than memory or assumption.

Pricing History

- Price lists used for exhibitions, open studios, fairs, or online platforms
- Gallery retail prices, including dates and venues
- Changes in pricing over time, with dates

Sales Records

- Invoices or receipts for completed sales
- Date of sale, artwork title or inventory number, and final sale price
- Buyer information when available or appropriate
- Notes on commissions or fees deducted

Discounts and Special Terms

- Collector or institutional discounts
- Friends-and-family pricing or bulk purchases
- Fundraising or benefit sales
- Any nonstandard terms affecting the final price

Appraisal Reports for Own or Owned Art

- Appraiser name and credentials
- Date and purpose of appraisal (insurance, estate, donation)
- Stated values and assumptions

Gallery and Consignment Documentation

- Consignment agreements
- Gallery statements showing retail price, commission, and net proceeds
- Records of returned or unsold work

How to Document and Organize
- Maintain one pricing and sales record per artwork, linked to the inventory number or title
- Use the inventory program or a simple spreadsheet to summarize pricing and sales history
- Attach or cross-reference scanned copies of invoices, price lists, and appraisals
- Name files clearly and consistently
- Record what occurred; do not revise prices or outcomes after the fact

Where to Store Information for Executor Access

Digital Storage

- Use the **ART ESTATE NAVIGATOR** in the Appendix to point an executor to the locations of documents
- An accurately labeled folder (e.g., Art Estate / Pricing & Sales)
- Cloud-based storage with shared or transferable access

Physical Storage

- A single binder or file box for original documents, in a protected, dry place

- Dividers for price lists, invoices, gallery statements, and appraisals

- Cross-references in the digital inventory noting where originals are kept

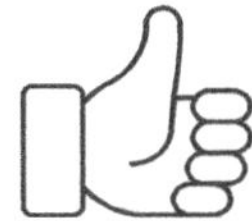

GOOD ENOUGH GUIDANCE

A partial, consolidated record is far more useful than scattered information.

COMPASS CHECK-IN

Which parts of your professional history, and the provenance of individual works, would be hardest for someone else to reconstruct without your input?

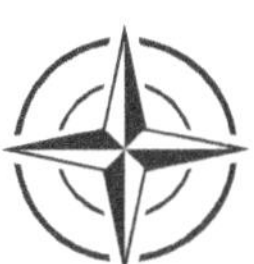

REMINDER: ART ESTATE NAVIGATOR

Take time to review and update the ART ESTATE NAVIGATOR. This review is intended to confirm your progress on the project. By now you've documented your art business, your inventory is underway or complete, and your professional contacts are accurately reflected. The updated worksheet will serve as the foundation for the executor instructions addressed in Step 8.

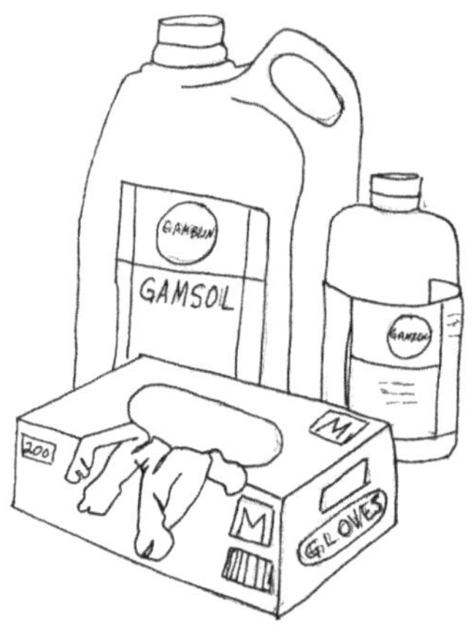

STEP 5: SECURE AND PROTECT YOUR ART BUSINESS

WHY THIS STEP MATTERS

Storage, insurance, and risk management must be considered whenever artwork is viewed as enduring. Artwork is vulnerable to environmental damage, loss, and disaster. Risk to the art business or estate increases significantly during periods of transition, when studios are disrupted and artwork is moved, stored, or handled by others. A single flood, fire, or prolonged climate failure can destroy decades of work.

Risk to artwork increases most during periods of transition, not just during disasters.

- Handling by untrained individuals, frequent movement, temporary storage, and delayed decision-making are among the most common causes of damage and loss.

- Administrative gaps—lapsed policies, unscheduled works, missing documentation—also create exposure

- Coverage should never be assumed to continue automatically

Finally, inaction itself is a risk. Prolonged uncertainty leads to repeated handling, unstable storage conditions, and cumulative damage. Even temporary holding periods require appropriate storage, insurance, and oversight.

CORE PRESERVATION FRAMEWORK

The following describes the essential considerations for the protection of your legacy.

Storage and Climate Control

Artwork should be stored in stable, climate-controlled environments whenever possible. Fluctuations in temperature and humidity accelerate deterioration, particularly for works on paper, textiles, photographs, and mixed media. Avoid basements, attics, exterior walls, and floor-level storage. Artwork should be elevated off floors, protected from direct sunlight, pests, and water intrusion, and housed in archival materials when appropriate. Off-site storage facilities should be selected for fine-art suitability, not general household storage. For higher-value works, specialized high-security fine-art storage facilities—including freeports and museum-grade art warehouses—offer advanced climate control, security, professional handling, and in some jurisdictions, bonded storage structures that may carry tax or customs implications.

Disaster Planning and Risk Mitigation

Disaster planning is essential to reduce preventable loss. Identify risks specific to the studio or storage site, including flooding, fire, storms, power outages, or building failures. Practical measures include elevating artwork, maintaining a current digital inventory stored off-site, and knowing how to speedily contact insurers, conservators, and storage facilities. Planning does not prevent disasters, but it determines whether damage becomes a total loss or a recoverable event.

Insurance Coverage

Standard homeowner or renter insurance rarely provides adequate coverage for artwork. Established artists with high-valued art, or individuals with estates with high-value art collections often require fine art policies or scheduled riders. Coverage should be reviewed to confirm what is insured, at what value, and under which conditions. Policies should extend to storage locations, transit, exhibitions, loans, theft, fire, water damage, and accidental loss.

Executors should locate all policy documents and notify insurers promptly following death or transition to confirm continued coverage.

Condition Reporting

Condition reports document the physical state of artwork and establish a baseline record. Reports typically include written descriptions and photographs noting surface condition, existing damage, framing, and mounting. Condition reports should be completed before and after loans, exhibitions, shipping, storage transfers, sales, or donations. Maintaining these records protects the estate by clarifying responsibility and supporting insurance claims if damage occurs. A more detailed description of condition reporting can be found in Step 3.

Coverage Scope and Limitations

Policies should be reviewed to confirm what risks are covered and under what conditions. Coverage should extend to:

- Primary and secondary storage location
- Transit and shipping
- Exhibitions and loans
- Theft, fire, water damage, and accidental loss
- Executors should verify exclusions, deductibles, and reporting requirements

Valuation and Documentation Requirements

Insurers may require inventories, appraisals, photographs, or condition reports to validate coverage and process claims. Confirm whether values are based on replacement cost, fair market value, or scheduled amounts, and whether updates are required over time.

Handling and Movement Risk

Risk increases substantially during studio clean-outs, property sales, temporary storage, and repeated handling. Executors should limit handling to designated individuals, avoid cleaning or altering artwork, and document conditions before and after any movement. Transit and short-term storage should be treated with the same care as long-term storage, including climate control and insurance coverage.

Digital records—including inventories, images, certificates, condition reports, and correspondence—should be backed up and accessible. Loss of documentation can significantly reduce value and complicate disposition.

Artwork is vulnerable to:
- Environmental failure
- Improper handling
- Gaps in insurance coverage
- Water exposure
- Unintended movement or access

When Immediate Protection Matters Storage, Insurance, and Risk Priorities. There are moments when a studio must be stabilized quickly — due to transition, relocation, health changes, or administrative shifts. In those early hours and days, the focus is not sorting, selling, or deciding. The focus is protection. A short delay can result in preventable damage — or unintended loss of coverage.

Notification and Continuity of Coverage. Executors should locate all policy documents and notify insurers promptly following death or transition. Some policies require notification to remain in force or to authorize executor control over insured property. Failure to notify can jeopardize coverage.

Visit the **APPENDIX: STORAGE, INSURANCE, AND CONDITION PROTEC-TION PROTOCOL** which outlines practical, time-sensitive priorities designed to: secure physical spaces; confirm climate stability; protect insured status; document condition before movement; preserve options for future decisions.

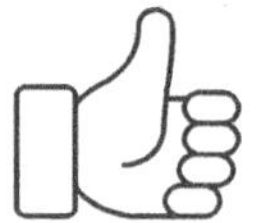

GOOD ENOUGH GUIDANCE

Artwork storage, insurance, and risk planning do not require perfection to be effective. The goal is to reduce preventable loss during periods of transition, not to create museum-level infrastructure. Stable climate conditions, basic insurance clarity, clear documentation, and limited handling are often sufficient to preserve artwork until long-term decisions are made.

If ideal storage or comprehensive coverage is not immediately available, prioritize the most vulnerable works first and focus on preventing exposure to water, extreme temperatures, and unnecessary movement. "Good enough" protection applied consistently is far more effective than delayed or incomplete action while waiting for ideal conditions.

COMPASS CHECK-IN

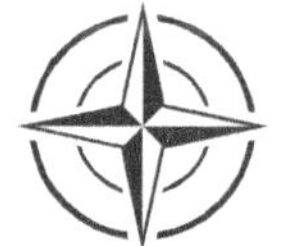

Before moving forward, confirm:

- Is the artwork currently stored in conditions that minimize environmental risk?

- Is insurance coverage confirmed, active, and appropriate for the current stage of transition?

- Is there documentation establishing conditions before any movement or handling?

- Are risks increasing due to delay, repeated handling, or temporary storage arrangements?

- If any answer is unclear, stop and stabilize conditions before proceeding. Preservation comes first. Decisions about sale, donation, or other disposition should move forward only once storage, insurance, and documentation are secure.

REMINDER: ART ESTATE NAVIGATOR

Complete the assessment of insurance and risk for your art practice. Review and update the ART ESTATE NAVIGATOR, and make any notes for discussions with an attorney, and executor instructions.

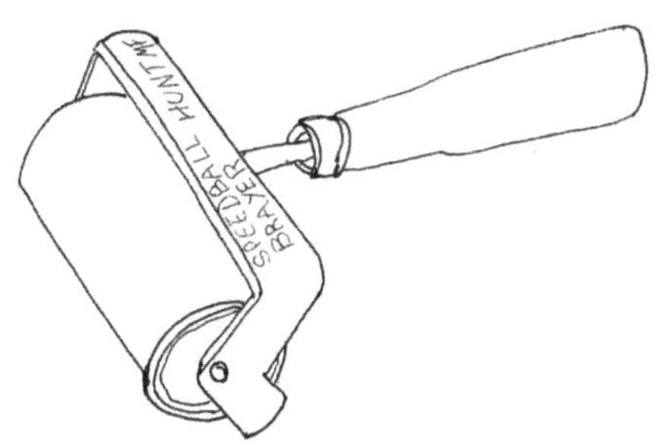

STEP 6: DOCUMENT DIGITAL ASSETS

WHY THIS STEP MATTERS

Digital assets are now an integral part of an artist's professional, financial, and historical footprint. Websites, social media accounts, online sales platforms, and paid digital tools may contain intellectual property, income streams, archives, client relationships, and records that exist nowhere else. Unlike physical materials, these assets can disappear when access is lost or accounts are left unmanaged.

When digital assets are undocumented, heirs or executors may be locked out entirely, accounts may be closed automatically, costly subscriptions may continue unnoticed, or decisions may be made without understanding the artist's intentions. Documenting digital assets is not about technology for its own sake—it is about preserving access, context, and choice.

ONE ARTIST'S EXPERIENCE

After a Seattle-based digital artist died unexpectedly, his family knew he had created and sold NFTs. They could see references to them on his website and social media, and they knew collectors had purchased the work. But no one could locate the private keys to his digital wallet. Without the password and authentication credentials, the NFTs could not be accessed, transferred, or sold. The works still existed on the blockchain—but for the family, they were effectively unreachable.

What might have represented significant value became, in practical terms, inaccessible.

Digital assets require the same clarity as physical ones: documentation of platforms used, wallet locations, authentication methods, and clear instructions for lawful access. Without that information, even visible and verifiable work can be lost to those left behind.

DIGITAL PLATFORMS

Begin by identifying and recording all digital platforms connected to the art practice in one place. This includes both public-facing platforms and behind-the-scenes tools used to support making, selling, communicating, marketing, or administering the work.

Common categories include:

- Websites and personal domains
- Blog, vlog or newsletters or other communication tools
- Social media accounts used professionally
- Online sales (Step 7 provides more information)
- Exhibit submission and portfolio platforms
- Design and writing tools
- Magazine subscriptions
- Payment platforms (Zelle, Venmo)
- Cloud storage
- Digital art
- Digital wallet and NFT platforms - (NFT- non-fungible tokens, a unique digital certificate recorded on a blockchain that verifies ownership and authenticity of a specific digital artwork.)

WHAT TO DO

Record Intentions

For each digital asset, note what should happen to it in the future. Some accounts may be intended to continue, others to be archived, and others to be closed. Chronicling intent allows others to act without guessing and helps prevent accounts from being shut down prematurely or left unattended.

Periodically review whether any website or blog domain that you use may have value beyond personal use. Does revenue come through either? In some cases, a domain name, what's used on the website, for example, may be an asset worth selling when a website is decommissioned.

Document Access

Access to online platforms should be stored securely, and its location specified. This does not require listing passwords publicly, but it should be clear to the executor where and how access credentials can be retrieved.

Note whether accounts use two-factor authentication, recovery email addresses, or phone-based verification, and identify who is authorized to retrieve access information. Note which websites or platforms have recurring subscriptions or credit cards attached.

NOTE TO EXECUTORS

For those stepping in after an artist's death, digital assets often provide essential clues about professional standing, income sources, and relationships. Websites, exhibit submission platforms and other online platforms may reflect exhibition history, audience reach, sales activity, or geographic ties that are not obvious from physical records alone.

If you are charged with disposition of artworks, do not decommission the website or social media properties until you have a strategy in place.

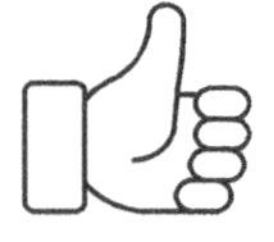

GOOD ENOUGH GUIDANCE

A simple list of platforms, general intentions, and clear access instructions is enough to complete this step. The goal is visibility and continuity, not technical mastery.

COMPASS CHECK-IN

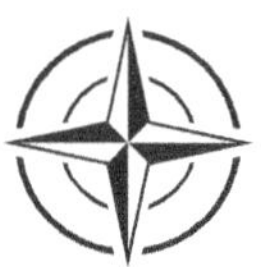

If someone unfamiliar with your art practice needed to step in tomorrow, would they know the extent of your digital presence, what should happen to those assets, and how to access them?

REMINDER: ART ESTATE NAVIGATOR

When you add your digital assets to the **ART ESTATE NAVIGATOR,** if your executor is not tech-savvy, consider providing explanatory notes.

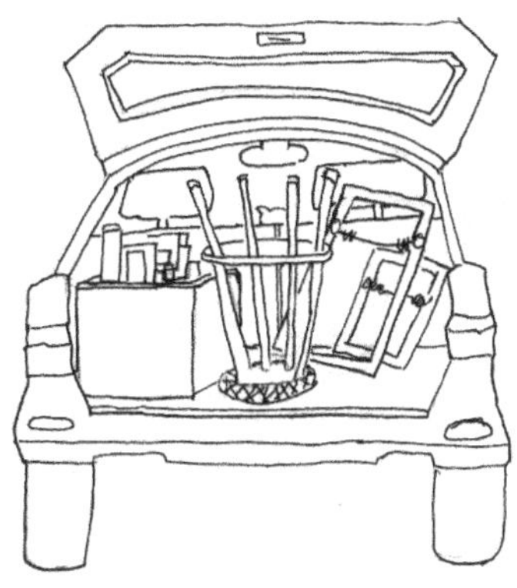

STEP 7: DOWNSIZING AND DISBURSEMENT OF THE ARTIST'S ARTWORK & STUDIO

WHY THIS STEP MATTERS

Finally, we've reached the part that likely triggered this entire project in the first place.

After all the organizing, documenting, clarifying of intent, and orienting yourself—and others—to the structure of the studio and estate, this is where decisions turn into action. For many artists and families, it carries the greatest sense of apprehension — the most emotionally charged and the most confounding. Decades of accumulated work must be faced directly. The jokes about "what will you do with all this?" become real questions. The physical evidence of a creative life demands resolution.

For artists whose work is spread across multiple locations—home studios, rented workspaces, storage units, foundries, shared facilities, or works on loan—this process must be repeated site by site, with careful coordination and consistent documentation.

If this feels like the real work at last, you are not wrong.

Step 7 is divided into three parts

Part 1: About Disposition — what to consider and how to start the disposition process.

Part 2: Disposition of Artwork — how finished and unfinished work is placed, sold, gifted, donated, reused, discarded, or destroyed. These decisions center on value, placement, legacy, and market context, and often require additional time, documentation, or professional input.

Part 3: About Disposition of Remaining Studio Contents — Supplies, equipment, tools, furniture, and books. Decisions about these materials are more practical than legacy-driven. The focus is on reuse or recycling, donation, or discarding, with greater attention to safety, space constraints, condition, and ease of handling, as described further below.

Step 7 is necessarily long. Unless the plan is a bonfire in the backyard or hauling everything away in a single day, doing justice to the disposition of artwork requires time, thought, sequencing, and often multiple simultaneous strategies.

- -

STEP 7 PART 1: ABOUT DISPOSITION

Disposition of the contents of an art studio is best approached as a sequence rather than a single decision. It usually unfolds over time rather than all at once. Some work may remain in active market channels, while other pieces move toward different forms of placement or release.

Beyond direct sales and gallery channels, when artwork is no longer intended for traditional sale, several distinct paths remain for moving items out of a studio. These options serve very different purposes and carry different implications for legacy, value, and responsibility. Understanding those differences is essential before taking action.

Protecting the Value of Art

A central goal in the disposition of artwork is to maintain—or, when possible, strengthen—the value and standing of the artist's work. This matters not only financially. It matters out of respect for the artist's career, for collectors who invested at full value, for institutions that exhibited the work, and for the broader historical context in which the work exists.

If your work has been collected, exhibited, or represented, how it reenters the world really does matter. Placing work thoughtfully—whether through an institutional gift or a structured sale—helps preserve its story and pricing history. Letting it drift into casual resale without attribution, into online marketplaces, flea markets, or other uncontrolled channels can unintentionally unsettle a market that may have taken decades to build.

No matter your reason for getting your studio in order, keep a list of resources you find and note them both in your contacts and records connected to your estate planning. Your heirs will appreciate this foresight.

Art Legacy Compass is based in Chicago, where there are many professional outlets and resources. In smaller communities, the landscape may look different. Options may be fewer, timelines longer, and creativity more necessary. Expectations may need to shift. Success may look different there—but thoughtful, responsible outcomes are still absolutely possible.

It's also worth saying something practical. Artists with formal representation, institutional exhibition history, higher-value work, and established collectors are simply more likely to generate meaningful financial return through sales. That isn't a judgment about artistic merit. It's just how art markets tend to function.

When the Goal of Disposition is Downsizing - Not Closing

For working artists building a professional presence, this is a reminder that continuing to build documentation, visibility, and relationships are not administrative extras; they directly shape your future options for continued growth in the art marketplace, and ultimately, your legacy. For hobbyists and community-based makers, the goal for your legacy and disposition may center more on meaningful gifts, local donations, or simply thoughtful distribution rather than through sales. For heirs and executors, understanding these distinctions helps set realistic expectations and focus energy where it will be most effective.

Even if you find yourself resonating with the idea of downsizing, this does not mean your art practice is in decline. It often reflects a desire to work more thoughtfully—not less, organize what you have, and strengthen the business side of your work. One eighty-year-old successful artist described his interest in decluttering not ending what he does but freeing him to try a new technique for his next series.

> Remove something from your studio today.

Whether prompted by an interest in revamping your art practice, a relocation, one too many stumbles over the buildup of finished and unfinished work, or consideration for heirs, downsizing requires decisions about what must be eliminated and where it can go. While the timeline may be flexible, success usually doesn't feel real until the studio feels lighter and easier to navigate, or until the work and materials can fit into a smaller, more manageable space.

Lean Into Your Community

While working through this project, lean into your art community. Art centers and specialty groups—such as pastel societies or quilting guilds—offer education, social connection, and exhibition opportunities. Building on these relationships and talking through the challenges and process with peers can generate new ideas, open additional channels for placement, and make the work feel lighter—perhaps you might create an annual art supplies sale or swap. Chances are someone else is staring at a stack of canvases and wondering what on earth to do next; compare notes, share a laugh, and move through it together.

ONE ARTIST'S EXPERIENCE

An artist's art space is often shared space—an office/exercise/studio, or a basement corner crowded with banker boxes of tax forms or a partner's passion project. One artist shared that as she and her husband planned to renovate the basement for her studio, the biggest challenge wasn't the construction—it was her partner's tendency to keep everything. EVERYTHING! This left little real room for her art practice.

Organizing and decluttering an art practice frequently involves other people and requires thoughtful, sometimes delicate, conversations to address concerns and set shared expectations.

Strengthen Your Art Practice

If your instinct is to pare down to rebuild, take an honest look at where your work stands in the wider world. If you are still actively making work, consider strengthening your professional footing. If you are preparing to wind down, think of this as clarifying and reinforcing the record of what you've done.

Research galleries—both in person and online—that handle work similar to yours. Visit them. Study the artists they represent. Pay attention to how they position work, price it, and communicate about it. If you are an emerging artist later in life, ask directly whether they represent emerging older artists. Many do.

The Patron Gallery in Chicago handles a 93-year-old painter who has been painting since graduating from the School of the Art Institute seventy years ago, and a 70-year-old painter who has been painting for fewer than fifteen years. Ballard's Fine Art Gallery in Sheridan, WY reached out to a talented 60+ Chicago artist. Age alone does not determine relevance or opportunity. What matters is the work, its quality, and its fit.

Expand your awareness of the field. Subscribe to a specialty magazine—digital or print—to stay current with conversations and trends. (Did you know there's a magazine devoted entirely to collage?) The more informed you are about where your work sits, the more strategic you can be about its future.

Use this moment not only to sort and place work, but to assess your professional footing. Strengthen your standing now—through careful documentation, increased visibility, meaningful relationships, and thoughtful placement of your work. And if you are closing your practice, these same efforts ensure that your work leaves your hands well documented, well positioned, and understood.

NOTE TO EXECUTORS

Honoring an artist's wishes means respecting the intent behind them—not executing them flawlessly. Written instructions and conversations should guide decisions, but they live within real-world limits. Time, cost, storage, safety, market conditions, and availability help all shape what is actually possible.

Executors and heirs are asked to act in good faith and make sound decisions—not to create perfect outcomes. Some estates prioritize efficiency and closure. Others focus on financial return or long-term legacy. Those priorities differ, and so do the strategies they require.

Sometimes that means resolving certain matters quickly while taking more time with others—selling some work to reduce costs, while holding key pieces for stronger placement. When exact wishes cannot be fulfilled, choosing the closest responsible path that honors the spirit of those wishes is both reasonable and appropriate.

With that understanding in place, the next step is to move from reflection into action by organizing the inventory to support clear decisions.

The Disposition Process

Sorting the Inventory into Disposition Categories

Before you start assigning destinations, make sure you can physically work.

If you're undertaking this project because you can't walk through your studio without tripping—or because every surface is covered—pause and create a small working zone. Even enough space for one person and a table or flat surface is sufficient. Remove obvious trash, empty boxes, and broken items first. This creates breathing room, both literal and psychological.

Sorting allows decisions to be made in stages, reducing the pressure to resolve everything at once. You can work through this task as you develop the inventory. The goal is to handle things minimally, so begin with broad categories; subcategories will be addressed later. Especially at the outset, it may take a few passes to feel confident about what belongs where.

Begin sorting into four broad categories: Here is a brief description of each. You will find more specifics below.

- **Donate:** Donations in the context of an artist's estate, is not the same as discarding an item to a thrift store. It refers to the intentional placement of artwork with an organization whose mission, audience, or collection aligns meaningfully with the work. This path prioritizes legacy, public access, education, or ethical considerations over financial return.

- **Gift and Personal Bequests:** Gifting and bequeathing artwork to family members, friends, or other heirs is one of the most meaningful forms of disposition. These transfers reduce inventory while preserving personal, cultural, and relational value—particularly when works hold family significance or reflect shared history. However, even the most dutiful, dedicated daughter or son will only want so much art.

- **Sell:** After all the time and financial investment, it's hoped there will be a return. In winding down, most likely comes from finished artwork, limited editions, quality frames, equipment, or studio tools with resale value. This may also include works that no longer represent your current direction but retain market interest. Be thoughtful about timing and pricing; not everything needs to be sold immediately.

- **Discard:** The last pile includes items that are broken beyond repair, expired, unsafe, mold-damaged, duplicated beyond usefulness, or no longer relevant to your practice. Old solvents, warped panels, unusable frames, dried paint, and outdated materials can be released, and yes, works you want destroyed.

Starting the Sort

- Work in small sections—one drawer, one shelf, one cabinet at a time.

- If you're unsure, put the piece in a temporary "Review" box and come back to it later. And remember the old food-handling rule: "When in doubt, throw it out."

- Attach sticky-notes with names and maybe a note for gifts to people or organizations.

- Attach color dots or sticky-notes to larger items to mark their destination.

- Photograph items slated for sale, donation, or gift (if not already documented) and update your inventory accordingly.

Sorting into these categories and seeing piles develop, gives a sense of the volume of items, but it does not require final decisions or commitments. It does provide the foundation for action. With an idea of the quantity of items, you are armed with a high level of info needed for conversations with various distribution sites.

Which sites require appointments for drop off? Will you need a box of garbage bags or a dumpster, a drawer or a storage shed? Should you rent a truck for a day, or borrow your daughter's minivan? How many frames are there to offer to an art center? Having an idea of the sheer volume, will help you make more efficient disbursement plans.

In practice, this sorting will change and become more specific as information improves, professional advice is received, or circumstances shift. That flexibility is intentional and protective.

At the end of every sorting and clean-out session, make it a point to remove discards from the studio. It will feel good and make more room to work.

ONE ARTIST'S EXPERIENCE

One artist, who lives a mile from a Salvation Army Family Store and Donation Center, created a ritual of walking a bag of give-aways there after clean-out sessions. He was unprepared for the nostalgia and grief he felt in letting go of art made fifty years earlier. The walk gave him time to process his emotions and plan his next session.

If at this point, you can also identify a likely destination or outlet for materials, all the better. Items intended for the same destination can then be grouped together. Identifying those that are going to be for sale, will make it easier to generate lists, or assemble a digital exhibition/viewing room.

NOTE TO EXECUTORS

Sorting enables progress without requiring deep familiarity with the artist's practice or market standing and creates natural pause points where professional guidance may be appropriate.

For some working through this process, it seems likely that sorting is going hand-in-hand with inventorying the contents of the studio and art practice. If you have no idea about the value of the work, find exhibition and sales records, and ask for help. If the artist took classes, connect with instructors. Google the artist, (really!) maybe it will give you a clue. Talk with an artist-friend of the decedent to get a sense of their standing.

STEP 7 PART 2: DISPOSITION OF ARTWORK

Each disposition pathway carries distinct practical and market implications, which are outlined below.

Donate Artwork

When an artist has an established professional presence—museum exhibitions, public commissions, strong regional recognition, or a loyal base of collectors—donation can be a thoughtful way to shape how the work is understood and remembered. Museums, universities, archives, and cultural organizations may welcome work that fills gaps in their collections, reflects local history, or supports teaching and research. Thoughtful placement helps ensure the work continues to be seen, studied, and valued. Successful donations typically involve:

- An existing or cultivated relationship with the organization

- Clear relevance between the artwork and the institution's mission or community

- Advance discussion about how the work will be used, stored, exhibited, or deaccessioned

For example, a sculpture of a baseball player may have relevance to a local stadium, or sports museum. Work connected to a region, teaching career, or social theme may resonate most strongly with local or affiliated institutions. Community hospitals, through their foundations, may accept work as a financial asset or fundraising tool, while hospitals with art therapy programs may have additional uses.

ONE ARTIST'S EXPERIENCE

After contacting the fundraising department of Memphis-based St. Jude Children's Research Hospital, one artist reported that he was surprised and pleased he was offered assistance to promote events where the proceeds would be donated to their organization. Don't be afraid to ask for assistance from the charity. Institutional donations are often the most deliberate and legacy-focused path, Like St. Jude, organizations are likely to make it easy for you.

Donation and Institutional Placement

Donation may involve placing artwork with museums, universities, nonprofits, or cultural organizations whose mission or audience aligns with the work. Acceptance policies vary, and all donations should be clearly documented for estate and tax purposes.

What differentiates them: Donation prioritizes legacy, access, and public value over financial return and is generally irreversible.

What to look for: Alignment between the artwork and the institution's mission, willingness to discuss how the work will be used or stored.

Who to contact:

- Museum curator
- Collections manager
- University archivist
- Art department chair
- Nonprofit executive director
- Foundation officer
- Board member or C-level

NOTE TO EXECUTORS

Disclaimer (Good-Faith Standard): Executors and heirs are not expected to secure ideal placements or guarantee preservation outcomes. The standard is to act in good faith, with reasonable care, documentation, and alignment with the artist's known wishes and professional standing.

When donation is pursued thoughtfully—based on available information, institutional interest, and practical constraints—it is considered responsible and appropriate, even when outcomes differ from the artist's hopes or expectations.

When legacy placement is not appropriate or feasible, volume-reduction options may still serve a practical role.

Gift and Personal Bequests

Personal bequests should be intentional, discussed when possible, and documented to prevent confusion or future conflict.

Specify the exact artwork or collection to be transferred for each beneficiary. Use clear titles, descriptions, dimensions, and inventory identification numbers so there is no ambiguity. If relevant, note any intentions—such as a desire for the work to remain within the family, to be displayed, or eventually donated.

When artwork has more than nominal value, lifetime gifting may carry tax implications. In 2026, an individual may give up to $19,000 per recipient per year without triggering federal gift tax reporting. Married couples may give up to $38,000 per recipient if they elect to split gifts. Gifts above these thresholds require the filing of a federal gift tax return, though tax is not owed unless lifetime exemption limits are exceeded. Gift tax limitations can change; artists should verify the rules in place at the time of the gift. Your executor or successor trustee should likewise confirm the applicable thresholds at the time of death or transfer.

Above all, personal bequests are a final creative decision. They're your way of deciding who will care for specific works—and why. Clear, thoughtful documentation—kept in your ART ESTATE NAVIGATOR helps ensure those choices are intentional, legally sound, and smoothly woven into your overall estate plan.

Recipients of gifted artwork typically assume the giver's cost basis, which may affect capital gains if the artwork is later sold. To reduce complications, artists and estates may consider spreading gifts over multiple years, transferring lower-value works, or consulting a qualified tax professional before conveying higher-value pieces.

Selling

There are many pathways for selling artwork, and they are often most effective when used in combination rather than in isolation. Different options support different price points, audiences, timelines, and levels of effort, and they can be adjusted over time as circumstances change. Existing gallery relationships are typically the first point of inquiry for existing artists, but other approaches are often needed to address the full scope of work. This section offers ideas for maximizing sales of artworks through the following:

- Gallery relationships

- Consignment

- Direct outreach

- Public and estate sales

- Online sales

- Auctions

Through any option, persistence and thoughtful decision-making still matter.

Gallery Relationships

For established artists, galleries where they are represented are the first place to turn when managing sales during a studio transition or estate process.

Galleries vary widely but can be broadly grouped into three types:

- Those that formally represent artists and actively promote their work to collectors

- Those that show and sell art without contractual representation

- Hybrid models that combine elements of both

When an artist has representation, the gallery often has a vested interest in sustaining the artist's reputation and value—even after the artist's lifetime. Galleries hold knowledge of collectors, past pricing history, and potential buyers that can be critical during transition.

Contracts should be reviewed carefully. Confirm whether the gallery is willing to represent some or all of the estate's work and document all terms clearly. Ask how pricing, storage, commissions, and timelines will be handled.

In some situations, a gallery may be willing to:

- Accept additional work on consignment

- Organize a retrospective, memorial exhibition, or limited-time presentation

- Feature the artist in a newsletter or online publication

Galleries place artwork through curated, relationship-based networks of collectors, institutions, and advisors. When a gallery promotes an artist's work they typically emphasize:

- Context

- Reputation

- Value and price stability

> Galleries focus on long-term positioning and narrative—not rapid liquidation.
>
> Representation may remain possible even if the artist is not actively producing work. However, some galleries may charge storage fees.

Unless the gallery has an exclusive on representing an artist, it may also be appropriate to identify additional galleries. It's important to question and perhaps revisit the exclusion; sometimes it's simply geographical — where the artist was prohibited from contracting with a gallery in the same town.

Gallerists report receiving hundreds of inquiries each month. One gallerist said she doesn't bother opening email inquiries, she prefers finding artists through her own means. Artists can get a gallerist's attention by approaching the organizations where their art fits by style, theme, or medium. Reading the "About" on the gallery website is the first clue. Reviewing the art and artists represented goes further. Visiting the galleries that seem to fit, chatting with the gallerists, having them ask to see your work, is the best. And, if asked, having strong images to show them is critical. Don't bother making broad casts of inquiries; prioritize and research finding a quality fit over broad outreach.

If a gallery represents an artist whose work is owned by the estate, a gallerist may also consider taking that piece on consignment for resale.

Consignment

Consignment describes both a type of relationship with an organization and a structure used by online platforms for selling work on behalf of an owner.

In a consignment arrangement, the owner places artwork with a gallery, dealer, or shop—to sell on their behalf. Ownership remains with the artist or estate until the work is sold. Once a sale occurs, the seller retains an agreed-upon commission, and the remainder is paid to the artist.

In an art context, consignment most often means that the artist or estate provides artworks to a gallery or dealer, who markets and sells the work under the terms of a written agreement. Payment is made only after a sale is completed

Direct Outreach

Selling directly to individuals is often one of the most productive and flexible strategies. It works within existing relationships and can be structured thoughtfully rather than rushed.

This may include:

- Notifying existing collectors of a studio closure or transition and offering early or priority access

- Reaching out to friends, colleagues, and local supporters already familiar with the work

- Contacting universities, colleges, or art centers where the artist studied, taught, or participated to explore exhibitions, retrospectives, or educational programs that may include sales.

- Monitoring social media and art publications for Calls-for-Art may occasionally present additional placement opportunities, though this approach is less likely to generate significant movement of work.

NOTE TO EXECUTORS

You Can Make a Difference

Take solace in the superpowers of an heir. Although scholars now believe that Vincent van Gogh sold only a handful of the nearly 900 paintings he created during his lifetime, his sister-in-law, Johanna van Gogh-Bonger—the wife of his brother Theo—was instrumental in establishing his reputation. She promoted his work through exhibitions, sold paintings strategically to build demand, and published the letters between Vincent and Theo. It can be done.

Public and Estate Sales

Public sales are generally more effective for reducing volume than for maximizing the value of major works. They require planning, staffing, and use of effective retail practices. One difference, not every piece must enter the market at the highest price point, but pricing decisions should not undermine collector confidence.

Public-facing options include:

- Renting a table or booth at a local fair, market, or holiday bazaar (well suited for prints, small works, cards, or editioned pieces)

- Hosting a closing studio sale or retrospective

- Producing a pop-up sale in partnership with a boutique

- Short-term rental of an empty storefront

- Scheduling an open studio event

- Including studio supplies, equipment, or furniture as part of the sale.

Estate sales function similarly and are typically best suited for dispersing:

- Prints

- Studies

- Lower-priced or minor works

In some cases, separating artwork from frames allows for more accessible pricing while offering frames to a different audience. However, this introduces handling risks that should be carefully considered. Before any public or estate sale:

- Separate and secure significant works

- Fully document and photograph major pieces

- Record original framing whenever possible

- Offer previously represented work to the appropriate gallery first.

Preparing Your Artwork for Sale

Selling artwork—whether through direct outreach, a studio event, or an estate sale—requires more than setting prices. It requires thoughtful positioning. How the work is presented, described, grouped, and handled influences how it is perceived and valued. Even in informal settings, preparation signals professionalism.

> Approach the sale as a temporary exhibition or retail store. The goal is to make viewing easy, the experience welcoming, while maintaining the value of the art.

Clear Communication

Provide visible, professional signage - at least 16-point font, readable from six feet away.

- Artist photo and short biography

- Clear statement that artwork is for sale and who benefits

- Title

- Medium

- Price

Create a guest book where visitors can leave comments and provide email addresses for follow-up. A simple thank-you note after a purchase reinforces goodwill and can be used in the event of additional sales.

Consider adding a QR code linking to available works, the artist's website, or a digital inventory. QR codes are easy to generate and allow buyers to review work without crowding tables. (Many plein air painters attach QR codes to their easels for exactly this reason.)

CREATE A GALLERY-LIKE EXPERIENCE

The gallery landscape has evolved in recent years. A number of commercial galleries have closed due to market pressures like rising costs, and changing buying habits toward lower cost art. New, smaller, independent galleries are opening, and new and inventive models are popping up.

In **New York,** a group of gallerists and artists parked U-Haul vans on the street, which were transformed into mobile pop-up galleries with hanging walls for paintings, plinths for sculptures and space for installations. The public is invited to step in and explore. In **Los Angeles,** artists converted an abandoned $.99 store into an affordable exhibition space. These low-investment, flexible venues make it possible to show and sell work without the burden of high overhead.

Let this be encouragement. You don't need a traditional gallery to begin. You don't need someone else to do it for you. Look around your own community and consider what's possible. With imagination and initiative, you can create opportunities that bring your work directly to people who want to live with it.

Before the Doors Open: Treat this like a retail event and develop 3-part strategy, Get People to:

1) Walk in

2) Look at a piece of art

3) Purchase it

1. WALK IN

Your contact list is an asset

- The artist's contact list is one of the most valuable tools in positioning a sale.
- Notify collectors directly
- Contact art centers and groups the artist participated in
- Announce the sale through social media
- Use local platforms such as Facebook Marketplace, relevant yard-sale groups, and Nextdoor to increase attendance
- Continue collecting email addresses—even if closing an art practice. When work sells through an exhibit, request buyer contact information when appropriate and follow up with a thank-you note. Personal communication builds goodwill and preserves relationships
- Create an invitational presale event for collectors
- Offer refreshments
- Shine attention on the artist with an artist talk, or stories about the artist

Curb appeal and signage

- Creative signage to get someone to interested
- Big letters and easy to read
- Coming soon signage

2. LOOK AT A PIECE OF ART

Merchandising: However you set-up your "gallery", it doesn't need to be expensive, but it should feel professional, intentional and orderly.

- Portable hanging walls for paintings and plinths for sculptures are available from rental centers, event and display companies, and sometimes galleries. Or create interesting fixtures, spray paint can do a lot for a metal shelving unit, old window frames, filing cabinet, or wooden ladder.
- Use eight-foot tables to accommodate works on paper and small paintings

- Group works by size (8"×10", 9"×12"), support (paper, panel, canvas), or framed/unframed status
- Framing is optional; many buyers prefer to choose their own
- Use shallow boxes (top removed, front lowered) to allow easy browsing of works on paper and panels
- For three-dimensional work:
  - Place glass and ceramics away from heavy foot traffic
  - Use removable gel or putty adhesives to secure objects safely
- Protect the condition of the work during handling:
- Package textiles, works on paper, and panels in protective sleeves or wrapping. One supplier to consider: www.clearbags.com
- Protective materials preserve condition and reinforce perceived value

Staffing: Ensure someone knowledgeable about the work is present during the sale

3. PURCHASE THE ART

You have visitors looking at the art. The goal is to encourage a purchase, maybe more than one, or make them a long-term collector.

- Make it easy for someone to buy the art.
- Price works consistently within size categories
- Avoid deep discounts that undermine prior collector values
- Offer modest incentives for multiple purchases if appropriate
- You will need a cash box with some cash. Consumers use Zelle and Venmo which makes the transaction easy. Your phone can work as a credit card reader with most services, but may need a business bank account. The bottom line is to support the transaction.
- Capture email addresses from customers for your thank you note and follow up emails for future interactions.

PROFESSIONAL ASSISTANCE

Some situations require practical, hands-on help with the physical work of managing a studio or home. These services provide operational support—assisting with organizing contents, installing artwork safely, and handling the logistics involved in selling or clearing materials.

Professional Art Preparators

Art preparators are trained installation professionals who handle, mount, and install artwork safely and correctly. They work with appropriate hardware, wall types, and weight requirements to ensure artwork is secure and properly supported. Preparators can also assist with placement and spacing so works are visually balanced while protected from damage.

What distinguishes preparators: Their expertise is the physical handling and safe installation of artwork.

What to look for: Experience installing artwork of similar size, weight, and medium, along with proper handling practices and tools.

Who to contact: A professional art preparator or installer, often referred by galleries, museums, art handling companies, or local arts organizations.

Estate Sale Professionals

Estate sale companies manage the sale of a home or studio's contents on behalf of an owner, heir, or executor. Services typically include sorting, staging, pricing, advertising, and running the sale itself. Their focus is efficient liquidation rather than fine art valuation or long-term placement. When artists' studios are involved, confirm that artwork will be identified and separated from general household items before pricing or sale.

What distinguishes estate sale companies: They specialize in clearing large volumes of household contents quickly and efficiently.

What to look for: Experience working with artist studios and clear policies that protect artwork from being treated as ordinary household goods.

Who to contact: A reputable estate sale company familiar with handling studio environments or artist estates.

Online Art Sales Platforms

Online platforms can play a useful role in selling artwork, but they are not interchangeable with traditional gallery, private, or auction sales.

Each operates under different market expectations and visibility conditions. The right choice depends on the artist's career context, the value of the work, and the executor's time and capacity.

Online sales are most effective when used selectively and in combination with other methods, rather than as a single solution.

Types of Online Art Platforms

Online art sales platforms offer additional channels for placement, but they operate under different market expectations than traditional galleries or private sales.

- **Dealer-Oriented Platforms**

  These platforms are restricted to established galleries and professional dealers. They typically feature higher-value work by established artists and operate within accepted market norms. Commission rates are often lower, but access is limited and usually requires an existing gallery relationship.

  Best suited for:
  Artists or estates already working within the primary art market and maintaining gallery representation.

- **Curated Online Marketplaces**

  In this model, the platform acts as the dealer. Artists apply for inclusion, and accepted work is presented within the platform's aesthetic and pricing framework. These platforms handle buyer communication and often shipping, in exchange for higher commissions.

  Best suited for:
  Independent artists without gallery representation and estates selling cohesive, well-documented bodies of work.
  Examples include UGallery, SINGULART, Artfinder, and Zatista.

- **Open Online Marketplaces (Self-Managed)**
  These platforms allow anyone to list work without review. Artists

or executors control pricing, presentation, and timing, but also carry the full burden of visibility, marketing, and accuracy. Quality and pricing vary, and the seller makes little after commissions. .

Best suited for:

Lower- to mid-value work, decorative pieces, or situations where reducing volume is more important than maximizing return.

Examples include Saatchi Art, eBay, and Chairish.

NOTE TO EXECUTORS

When Online Platforms Make Sense—and When They Don't

Online platforms can be helpful, but they are not neutral. Once work is publicly listed with visible pricing, it enters a permanent digital record that can affect future sales, perceived value, and legacy.

Online platforms are most appropriate when:

- The artist leaves guidance supporting public online sales
- Works are mid-range or decorative rather than historically significant
- Speed, convenience, and volume reduction are priorities
- The executor has time to manage listings, communication, and follow-through

Online platforms should be avoided or used cautiously when:

- Works were previously sold through galleries at established price points
- The artist's market relies on controlled placement or private sales
- Documentation, attribution, or condition reporting is incomplete
- The executor lacks time to manage pricing, inquiries, disputes, or returns

Before committing to any online platform, confirm:

- Commission and fee structure
- Who is responsible for photography, packing, and shipping
- Payment timing and return policies
- Dispute resolution procedures
- Time commitments and listing expiration rules

Auctions

Auction houses sell artwork through competitive bidding, either in live rooms, online, or in hybrid formats. Prices are established publicly by buyer demand at a specific moment in time rather than through negotiated asking prices. This structure can be powerful—but only when the artist's market context supports it.

Auctions are most effective for artists whose work is already recognized by collectors and has a documented sales history. For established artists, auction results can confirm market position and create liquidity. For others, the same transparency can expose uneven demand and lock in prices that are difficult to reverse.

Established Artists and the Auction Market

For artists with established careers—those with consistent exhibition histories, institutional recognition, or a record of gallery and private sales—auction houses can serve as a validation mechanism rather than a discovery platform.

Auction houses generally expect:

- Prior sales through galleries, private dealers, or institutions
- A consistent body of work that fits recognizable categories or periods
- Clear documentation, provenance, and condition records

How Auctions Differ from Other Sales Channels

Unlike online galleries or consignment platforms, auctions prioritize speed, transparency, and finality. Works are offered within a fixed sales cycle, with published estimates and permanent public results. Once consigned, the seller has limited control over pricing, buyer selection, or placement.

Key characteristics include:

- Pricing is public, negotiation happens prior to auction
- Fixed timelines driven by auction calendars

- Limited flexibility once consignments of art are accepted

- Permanent visibility of results, including unsold lots, (meaning, if an artist's work isn't sold, it can be viewed negatively.

- For established artists, this visibility can either reinforce credibility or introduce volatility. Following the results of an auction, reassessing pricing is a must.

When Auctions Are Most Effective:

- Comparable works by the artist have sold successfully in recent years

- Demand exceeds supply for specific bodies of work

- The auction house already serves collectors aligned with the artist's medium and scale

- Individual market-ready works are offered, rather than entire studio contents.

Choosing the Right Auction House

Beyond major international firms, many regional and specialty auction houses actively sell works by established local and regional artists, often with better contextual knowledge and more focused collector bases.

To identify auction houses that might fit your needs, visit platforms that aggregate auctions from regional to worldwide, and show past results of sales and pricing patterns. www.LiveAuctioneers.com is a good example.

Who to Contact: Email, call or visit an auction house to identify the specialist for the genre, or a general consignment director. They will likely want photos first, and suggest a visit to see the art. Because they are interested in making sales, they should address risks as well as opportunities and will not encourage consignments just to fill a sale.

Charity Auctions vs. Commercial Auctions

Charity auctions are designed to raise funds for an organization, not establish market value. Bidding is often influenced by goodwill and social context rather than sustained collector demand. While a high charity result can look positive, it creates risk for an artist: once a price is set publicly, comparable works are expected to align with it—even if the broader market will not support that level. This can leave an artist or estate with inflated expectations and limited real demand. On the other hand, it doesn't hurt the artist's reputation, and it can bring visibility to them, but a charity auction should be used cautiously and not treated as reliable indicators of market value.

> **Conducting Your Own Auction**
>
> If the artist has a following, consider holding your own auction series online. Set a consistent time each month or week, to "drop" the next auction item. Offer an artwork at a minimum price that is 50% lower than regular prices. Take the best offer after five days. Then repeat. Post an image on the website. Promote your personal auction across socials and send links to collectors, friends and family.

If it's decided to donate a work to a charity auction, the context of the sale should be noted in the inventory.

PROFESSIONAL ASSISTANCE

As artwork moves from planning into active sale, professional guidance can shape outcomes in important ways. For established artists in particular, the goal is rarely just to sell work—it is to place it thoughtfully, protect value, and avoid actions that unintentionally disrupt a market built over many years. The right professionals can help streamline decisions, reduce risk, and prevent costly missteps.

While the general roles in the art market are widely understood, the boundaries between them are often fluid. Before seeking help, take time to clarify the problem you are trying to solve.

WHO DOES WHAT IN THE ART MARKETPLACE

Professional	Primary Role	Typical Clients	When They Are Most Helpful
Art Agent	Represents the artist's business interests	Artists, sometimes estates	Managing opportunities, commissions, and professional negotiations
Art Advisor	Provides independent guidance on value, placement, and strategy	Collectors, families, estates	Evaluating a body of work and deciding what to sell, keep, donate, or place
Art Dealer	Buys, sells, or brokers artwork to collectors	Artists, collectors, estates	Placing individual works with collectors already active in the market
Art Consultant	Sources artwork for design projects	Corporations, designers, developers	Placing work in hotels, offices, healthcare facilities, and large projects

Art Agents

Art agents represent the business interests of artists. Less common than gallery representation, agents help manage opportunities, negotiate agreements, and expand professional connections. They may arrange commissions, negotiate licensing or reproduction rights, coordinate exhibitions, or secure institutional and commercial opportunities. For artists with active markets, an agent can manage the professional side of the work so each opportunity does not have to be negotiated independently.

What distinguishes agents: They advocate for the artist's professional and financial interests across multiple opportunities.

What to look for: A clear written agreement outlining scope of representation, commissions, and whether the agent has exclusivity.

> **Who to contact:** An agent experienced with artists working in similar mediums, markets, or career stages.

Art Advisors

Art advisors help collectors, artists, families, and estates make informed decisions about artwork. They typically do not buy or sell work themselves but provide independent guidance on value, market context, and placement options. Advisors may evaluate a body of work, help determine which pieces might be sold, donated, or retained, and recommend appropriate galleries, dealers, or auction venues. For complex estates or large bodies of work, they provide an objective perspective on timing, pricing, and placement.

> **What distinguishes advisors:** They focus on evaluation and strategy rather than direct sales.

> **What to look for:** Transparent fees, independence from specific sales outlets, and strong knowledge of the artist's market segment.

> **Who to contact:** An independent art advisor or advisory firm experienced in the artist's field, medium, or regional market.

Art Dealers

Art dealers buy, sell, or broker artwork independently and often operate outside formal gallery structures. They are strategic matchmakers who connect specific works with collectors already active in the market. Unlike galleries, which emphasize long-term representation, dealers tend to work more transactionally and flexibly, placing individual works or identifying niche buyers when demand aligns. Used selectively, experienced dealers can help place work without committing an entire body of work to a single outlet.

> **What distinguishes dealers:** They prioritize timing and opportunity over long-term representation.

> **What to look for:** Clear explanations of pricing, commissions,

resale intent, and how sales may affect existing gallery relationships or collector expectations.

Who to contact: An independent or private dealer with demonstrated experience in the artist's marketplace.

Art Consultants

Art consultants source and place artwork for businesses, designers, and institutions. Their focus is selecting work that fits a specific project, space, or budget. Consultants often purchase artwork for hotels, healthcare facilities, corporate offices, residential developments, and other design-driven environments, sometimes placing multiple works at once.

What distinguishes consultants: They match artwork to design projects rather than building an artist's collector market.

What to look for: Clear pricing, defined project parameters, and confirmation that artwork will be properly credited when installed.

Who to contact: An art consulting firm or independent consultant working with corporate, hospitality, healthcare, or architectural clients.

For many estates, an art advisor or appraiser is often the first professional consulted before deciding whether work should be sold through dealers, galleries, or auctions.

Recycling Artwork

When work cannot be placed, sold, or retained, recycling offers a responsible alternative to conventional disposal.

Reuse is irreversible. When preservation, legacy, or future value is uncertain, the safest decision is to retain the work unchanged. Reuse, reworking, or transformation can be practical, creative, and sometimes emotionally relieving options.

ONE ARTIST'S EXPERIENCE

A highly prolific 78-year-old artist made a simple but deliberate decision: for every new painting he began, he would return to one he had previously set aside.

The results surprised him. First, he began to see—with a kind of quiet satisfaction—how his style had evolved over time. Revisiting earlier work sharpened his awareness of what he was doing now and helped him paint with greater intention. Second, many of those older pieces were brought forward into his current language. By reworking them, he aligned them more closely with the style his collectors recognized and expected. And third, something practical happened. His overall output increased, and the stack of unfinished or unresolved paintings began to shrink. Inventory that would otherwise have required future decisions gradually resolved itself.

A simple discipline accomplished three things at once: artistic awareness, stronger market alignment, and fewer works left to manage later.

Collage and Assemblage as Creative Transformational Recycling

Beyond reuse, artists may choose to transform parts of existing works—paintings, sculpture fragments, textiles, or studio remnants—into new collage or assemblage pieces. This approach reframes earlier work not as something to be corrected or erased, but as material with history, texture, and meaning.

For many artists, collage and assemblage offer an emotionally and creatively satisfying alternative to disposal. This method is particularly well suited to mixed media practices and aligns with growing cultural interest in sustainability, recycling, and material reuse.

> From a studio management and legacy perspective, creative transformation can be a deliberate way to reduce volume while continuing to make meaningful work.

NOTE TO EXECUTORS

In preparing an estate, the artist may provide guidance and authorization for reuse or changing their work. Executors should not authorize reuse, reworking, dismantling, or material salvage unless the artist has explicitly directed reuse or the work has been specified as non-preservation material. Reuse decisions are final. Even unfinished, unsold, or storage-intensive works may hold future value that is not immediately apparent.

When uncertainty exists, the safest course is to retain the work unchanged and seek guidance from the artist's records, a trusted advisor, or a qualified art professional before approving alteration or disposal.

Discard

Discarding artwork is sometimes necessary, but it should be approached deliberately rather than reactively. Some work will not be placed, sold, or retained. Discarding, whether through destruction or responsible recycling, requires deliberate judgment.

Thrift Stores

Thrift stores serve charitable missions. They accept donated goods, price them for quick turnover, and move inventory efficiently to support community programs. Within the context of an artist's studio or estate, however, thrift stores function as a volume-reduction mechanism—not as a legacy strategy.

Artwork placed in thrift stores is typically:

- Priced for rapid sale

- Sold without attribution, provenance, or context

- Removed from established gallery or collector channels

- Detached from prior pricing history

Once on a thrift store floor, a painting becomes décor. A sculpture becomes an object. The market narrative surrounding the work—its exhibition history, its placement among collectors, its relationship to the artist's larger body of work—disappears.

For artists with an established market presence, gallery representation, or active collectors, this matters. Work released into uncontrolled resale environments can undermine pricing consistency and perceived value. Collectors who paid full market price may later encounter similar works for a fraction of that amount, without explanation. Even if the work was minor or experimental, the signal to the market can be confusing.

For this reason, thrift donation should be approached cautiously when dealing with professionally exhibited, cataloged, or actively collected work. In most cases, it should be considered a last resort for pieces with recognized market history.

That said, thrift stores can be entirely appropriate for:

- Student or practice pieces
- Decorative work with no established market
- Studies or minor works
- Frames and framing materials

For artists without an established collector base—particularly hobbyists or community artists—thrift stores may be a practical and even positive destination. In many communities, donated artwork is purchased to furnish homes, seasonal residences, or offices. In some stores, frames are routinely reused by working artists.

A Courtesy to Living Artists

When heirs or executors are handling artwork created by a living artist, it is often wise to contact the artist before donating, reselling, or discarding the work.

Even when legal ownership has transferred, offering the artist the opportunity to reclaim or repurchase the piece respects the artist's ongoing relationship to their work. It may prevent unintended damage to reputation or market standing. Many artists would rather reacquire their own work than see it circulate casually.

This gesture is not legally required. It is professional courtesy.

Location matters: stores in affluent or tourist areas may sell artwork more readily than others.

> Discarding artwork is not failure. It is discernment. It is the final edit of a body of work.

Intentional Destruction: Final Editing of the Work

After reasonable efforts at sale, gifting, donation, and archive placement have been explored, some artwork will remain. Studies that never resolved. Experimental pieces that failed. Damaged works. Duplicates. Pieces that no longer represent the artist's standards or vision.

> More than one artist has described the destruction of unsuccessful work as unexpectedly liberating. For many artists, choosing what will endure—and what will not—is an affirmation of authorship. It is control exercised thoughtfully, not recklessly. It is closure chosen, not imposed.
>
> One spoke of slicing through canvases that had lingered for years, calling it "the cleanest critique I ever gave myself."

Allowing such works to circulate informally—especially through thrift stores or uncontrolled channels—can create confusion in the marketplace and among collectors. In some circumstances, intentional destruction becomes the clearest and most responsible choice.

Artists have long exercised the authority to cut apart canvases, dismantle sculptures, or deconstruct mixed-media works that no longer belong in their oeuvre. The act is practical. It prevents unfinished or unsuccessful work from reentering circulation. It removes ambiguity for heirs. It affirms authorship.

Materials may be recycled where possible or responsibly discarded through appropriate waste channels. Photographs can be retained in the inventory record to document that the decision was deliberate and aligned with the artist's intent.

PART 3: DISPOSITION OF REMAINING STUDIO CONTENTS

Supplies, Equipment, and Tools

Disposition of studio materials requires the same intentional thought as the disposition of artwork itself. While some artists prefer to address tools, equipment, furnishings, and supplies at the same time they are placing artwork, this process can also be handled separately. In many cases, the destinations overlap—art centers, educational institutions, and art recycling centers may accept both artwork and certain studio assets. The key is to approach the contents of the studio systematically, recognizing that materials often hold financial, practical, or archival value.

Disposition Paths for Studio Materials:

- Sale of equipment or furnishings (presses, kilns, easels, flat files, lighting, shelving)

- Gifting to assistants, students, colleagues, or family members

- Donation of usable supplies to schools, community art centers, nonprofits, or educational programs

- Recycling or creative reuse of materials through local reuse centers

- Discard of broken, hazardous, or unusable items

Before dispersal, photograph the space, inventory specialized tools, and retain manuals, warranties, or technical notes that may be useful to future owners. For large or complex studios, professional cleanout or estate services may be appropriate to ensure safe and efficient handling of the items besides artwork.

Selling Supplies, Equipment, and Furniture

These items can be sold with or separately from the art and may be promoted through some of the same channels, particularly when they are of interest to other artists. Online platforms can be effective, such as Facebook Marketplace, Nextdoor, and eBay, especially for local pickup or specialized tools.

If the artist has been active in an art center or community organization, it may be possible to:

- Organize an art materials sale at that location

- Invite other artists to participate

- Structure the event as a fundraiser for the artist or the artist's family

Announcements may also be shared through art center newsletters or community mailing lists. Group or community-based sales can reduce effort, increase turnout, and build goodwill while helping clear a studio efficiently.

Sales of non-art assets should be documented carefully. Any required permissions, approvals, or estate authorizations should be confirmed in advance, and clear financial records should be maintained.

No matter how the work is sold, results are better when you intentionally reach out to your full network.

Maximizing Networks: All sales approaches benefit from activating the artist's network, including collectors, fellow artists, art organizations, friends, family, former students, and collaborators. Personal outreach often results in more thoughtful placement of work than anonymous listings and helps ensure that work is placed with individuals or institutions that value its significance.

It is helpful to decide in advance how long and how deeply to remain involved in the sales process.

Recycling Studio and Non-Art Materials
(Paints, supplies, equipment, and furniture—not finished artwork)

Recycling and reuse are ethical and practical ways to keep usable materials in circulation when they are safe, identifiable, and stable. Some organizations that accept artwork may also accept certain supplies; confirm directly before delivering materials.

Who May Benefit

- Other working artists

- Emerging artists

- Art teachers and school programs

- Community art centers

- Senior centers

- Park districts

- Creative reuse organizations

Materials that often retain reuse value include:

- Partially used paints and mediums

- Clearly labeled open containers of supplies

- Scraps and test pieces

- Unusual papers or substrates

- Usable tools and studio hardware

Reuse is appropriate only when materials are usable, specifically labeled, and safe. Unsafe, unlabeled, contaminated, or deteriorating materials should not be passed on.

The non-art items in a studio are often the most physically demanding and safety-sensitive part of downsizing. Decisions are typically guided by volume, logistics, and safety rather than maximizing financial value.

For artists, letting go of materials may reflect changing methods or a reduced scale of work—not an end to making art.

Hazardous Studio Materials: Safety First

Some studio materials are unsafe to reuse, recycle, or dispose of casually. This guidance applies to both artists and executors.

Hazardous materials should never be placed in household garbage or recycling or poured down drains. Executors and heirs are not expected to identify or test hazardous substances. Choosing safe disposal is a responsible act.

Common hazardous materials include:

- Oil-soaked rags
- Unlabeled liquids
- Solvents
- Acids
- Powdered pigments

Disposition Option: Municipal and Household Hazardous Waste Programs

Municipal waste departments and Household Hazardous Waste programs handle materials that are unsafe to discard casually.

Their purpose: Protect people, buildings, and infrastructure; not recover value

What to confirm before delivery:

- Drop-off schedules
- Volume limits
- Handling instructions

Who to contact:

- Municipal waste or environmental services department

Creative Reuse and Community Redistribution

Established creative reuse organizations redirect usable studio materials—including paints, tools, supports, and supplies—back into circulation. Their focus is material recovery and redistribution, not artistic legacy, valuation, or finished works.

Creative reuse organizations generally:

- Recover usable materials

- Redistribute supplies

- Support community access and sustainability

- They do not assess authorship, provenance, or long-term legacy considerations.

- These programs are generous and impactful options—but they are never obligations.

There are programs and reuse centers that accept donated art supplies and studio materials, often at no or low cost (policies vary by location and condition). Some operate independently; others are part of broader networks that collect and redistribute surplus art, craft, and design materials.

Before delivering materials, confirm that the center has:

- Clear acceptance lists (types, quantities, condition)

- Safety requirements for paints, solvents, aerosols, or sharp tools

- Defined drop-off procedures and scheduling

- Restrictions on hazardous items

An up-to-date list of national and regional resources can be found at www.artlegacycompass.com.

> **Create Your Own Reuse Event**
>
> You may choose to organize a sell, swap, or donation event in partnership with a local art center, community studio, or nonprofit organization. These events can be especially effective during studio closures or downsizing. They build creative community while reducing waste.
>
> When organizing such an event:
>
> - Work with an established host to manage space, safety, and logistics
>
> - Set clear guidelines about accepted materials
>
> - Distinguish supplies from finished artwork
>
> - Consider combining sales, swaps, and free donation tables
>
> - Invite teachers, park districts, and community art directors

Disposition of Studio Furniture and Large Equipment

Large studio furniture and equipment require additional planning because of their size, weight, and potential value. Items such as tab-orets, high-end easels, shelving systems, television monitors used for reference or display, and kilns may be expensive, specialized, or difficult to transport. These pieces can be handled alongside artwork disposition or separately, depending on logistics.

The three most likely places to approach are:

- Local art centers or community studios
- University or community college art departments
- Established artists or teaching studios in your region

When approaching these organizations or individuals:

- Contact the program director or department chair directly with a clear description, dimensions, condition report, and photographs.
- Be transparent about timing and whether pickup is required.
- Clarify whether the item is a gift, sale, or tax-deductible donation, and request written acknowledgment if applicable.

Advance communication and complete information make it far more likely that substantial equipment will find an appropriate next home.

Disposition of Books

Shelves of artists' studios bend under the weight of books: exhibition catalogs, artist monographs, technique manuals, art history texts, theory, philosophy, poetry, novels, notebooks, and dog-eared paper-backs picked up years ago and never quite released. These books are not background décor. They are tools, teachers, companions, and witnesses to a working life. They hold the thinking behind the making: influences absorbed, problems solved, directions abandoned and rediscovered. Together, they form an intellectual map of how an artist learned, experimented, and came to see the world.

Artist Monographs

Artist monographs are in-depth books that tell the story of an artist's life, career, or a focused period of work within a genre. They usually include high-quality images, biographical background, critical essays or art historical analysis, exhibition history, and bibliographic information.

Because of this depth and documentation, monographs often hold the strongest long-term value among studio books and can be collectible.

In downsizing, monographs that meaningfully influenced the artist's work or reflect important affinities are often worth keeping selectively; others may be strong candidates for donation to libraries, schools, or peers.

Exhibition Catalogs

Exhibition catalogs carry high documentary and legacy value but uneven market value. Their importance lies in what they substantiate: where and when work was exhibited, who presented it, and how it was contextualized at a given moment. For artists, heirs, executors, and appraisers, catalogs serve as credible third-party records supporting exhibition history and provenance.

> Books present a particular challenge. They are heavy with meaning but uneven in practical value, and they accumulate faster than they leave. Not every book needs to be saved, but few can be dismissed casually. Decisions about what to keep, pass on, donate, sell, or discard demand careful consideration.

Resale value is typically modest unless the catalog is tied to:

- A major institution
- A historically significant exhibition
- A widely recognized artist

In downsizing, catalogs that document the artist's own work or key career milestones are often worth retaining selectively, while duplicates or minor group exhibitions may be appropriate for donation or release.

Technique Manuals and How-To Books

Technique manuals are primarily functional tools rather than legacy objects, and their value is usually practical, time-bound, and personal. They reflect how an artist learned to work—materials explored, processes tested, and problems solved—but they rarely carry significant market value once superseded by newer methods or technologies.

Their greatest usefulness often lies in active studios, classrooms, or among emerging artists who can put them to immediate use. When reducing a studio, manuals that document unusual, obsolete, or specialized techniques may be worth retaining briefly for reference or transfer to a student or colleague, while more common or outdated titles are appropriate for donation or release without concern.

Artists and executors can sell higher-value monographs, exhibition catalogues, and technique books to a reputable secondhand bookstore—especially one that specializes in art—or through online marketplaces where collectors search for out-of-print titles. Donation options include local art centers, university art departments, community colleges, museum study libraries, or nonprofit groups that support artists; some women's art organizations or university women's centers may also welcome relevant materials. Before donating, it's wise to confirm what subjects and quantities they will accept.

Discard Non-Artwork: Materials, Equipment, and Remaining Studio Contents

Decisions about non-artwork should be based on practical criteria:

- Safety

- Condition

- Usability

- Completeness

- Storage cost

- Environmental compliance

Broken equipment, obsolete technology, dried or contaminated materials, unlabeled chemicals, unstable shelving, and unusable furniture should not be redistributed. If an item cannot be safely used, responsibly recycled, or appropriately donated, it should be discarded.

Executors are not required to retain tools or supplies indefinitely. Heirs are not obligated to store materials that no longer serve a function. The objective is safe and orderly resolution.

Materials in good condition may be donated to community art centers, schools, university departments, or other appropriate organizations. However, donation must not transfer risk.

> **Permission Statement**
>
> You are allowed to:
> - Stop selling before everything is sold
> - Shift from sale to donation or gifting
> - Recycle or responsibly discard items that no longer serve
> - Handle different categories through different channels

Hazardous materials must be disposed of according to local environmental regulations. Electronics should be sent to certified e-waste facilities. Chemicals require proper hazardous waste handling.

When disposal is necessary, it is a standard administrative decision—not a failure.

Final Considerations

Documentation: Depending on the estate, only disposal of significant items should be recorded in the inventory or administrative file. It's best if the artist identifies what shouldn't be destroyed. Documentation should include:

- General category of item
- Approximate quantity
- Date of disposal
- Method of disposal (recycling, hazardous waste, landfill, etc.)
- Photographs may be retained when appropriate.

This record demonstrates that decisions were deliberate and properly managed.

Removal and Completion: Once sorting decisions are made, discarded items should be removed promptly. Whenever possible, disposal should occur at the end of each working session to prevent re-accumulation.

Clearing unusable materials simplifies inventory, reduces storage costs, and allows remaining assets to be managed efficiently.

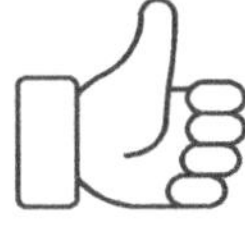

GOOD ENOUGH GUIDANCE

This step is about choosing and following a small number of realistic paths to reduce or dispose of the artist's estate. Its success comes with:

- Setting clear limits on time, scope, and expectations
- Accepting that not every strong piece will sell—and that this is normal
- At this stage, success can be measured by revenue, or maybe, more by:
- Work leaving the studio with intention
- Reduced physical and mental burden
- Clear documentation of what was offered, where, and why
- A good-enough approach usually includes:
- One primary channel (existing gallery, personal network, or online presence)
- One secondary outlet (studio sale, consignment, or limited public offering)
- Clear pricing logic, even if imperfect (consistent tiers beat endless recalibration)
- A defined stopping point (date, number of works, or energy limit)

NOTE TO EXECUTORS

Good Enough" means:

- Following documented guidance rather than optimizing outcomes
- Avoiding speculative pricing or unfamiliar markets
- Knowing when to pause, regroup, or shift unsold work to another disposition path

If disposition of the studio or estate begins to require constant reworking, justification, or emotional strain, it is no longer serving its purpose. That is your signal to stop, not push harder.

This step is successful when:

- Decisions can be explained with ease

- The process is repeatable or transferable

COMPASS CHECK-IN

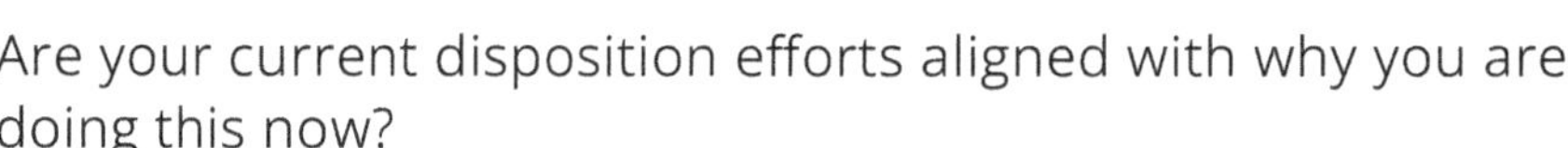

Orientation Question:

Are your current disposition efforts aligned with why you are doing this now?

Can someone else reasonably understand the strategy and tactics for disposing of some or all of the contents of an art life?

Energy Test:

- After engaging in any disposition activity—selling, coordinating donations, arranging gifts, or organizing removal—do you feel:
- Some relief or clarity → keep going
- Drained, resentful, overwhelmed, or stalled → reassess the channel, the scale, or the timing, and/or ask for help

REMINDER: ART ESTATE NAVIGATOR

With the planning work in this guide now substantially complete, take time to review and update the **ART ESTATE NAVIGATOR.**

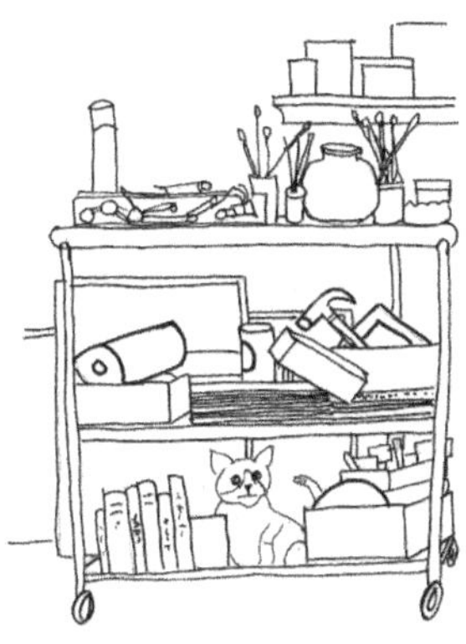

STEP 8: PREPARE INSTRUCTIONS FOR YOUR EXECUTOR

WHY THIS STEP MATTERS

Up to now, you have been planning. In this step, you make that plan usable.

Earlier Steps helped you clarify your intent, build an inventory, organize records, identify income streams, evaluate sales or donation options, and reduce studio materials. You made those decisions with time and perspective.

Your executor will not have that luxury.

This step is where you turn your decisions into clear written instructions, so your executor does not have to guess, interpret, or reconstruct your thinking.

WHO THIS STEP IS FOR

This step is written for you — the artist.

Your executor may not be an art professional, familiar with your studio systems, comfortable interpreting market conditions, or interested in redesigning your strategy.

You are not asking them to decide what should happen. You are telling them what you have already decided — and how to carry it out.

HOW EXECUTOR INSTRUCTIONS WORK

Your will or trust grants legal authority — meaning the formal right to act on your behalf.

Your Executor Instructions explain how you want that authority used in relation to your artwork and other studio contents, archives, and income-producing arrangements.

DEVELOPING YOUR EXECUTOR INSTRUCTIONS

Throughout the previous Steps, you have been completing your **ART ESTATE NAVIGATOR,** documenting the full scope of your art practice and art estate.

> Executor Instructions provide priorities, boundaries, and practical direction.
>
> Think of them as the operating manual for the plan you built.

The Appendix includes the **EXECUTOR PACKET — ART ESTATE ADMINISTRATION GUIDE.** This packet acts as a cover and roadmap for your executor to use. It organizes tasks by timeframe and topic so the work unfolds in a logical order, and resources to make it easy.

For example, it helps clarify authority (who is empowered to act and when), stabilization (what must be secured or protected immediately, such as locking studio spaces or confirming insurance), financial safeguards, how to confirm and use the inventory, how to protect provenance and documentation, boundaries around sales, gifts, donations, or destruction, and suggested communication templates.

Art Legacy Compass is here to help you think through decisions and get organized. It is not a substitute for legal advice or estate planning documents. Please consult an attorney to ensure your wishes are properly documented and legally enforceable. The Appendix provides structure; your instructions provide the content.

Personal Bequests

If you wish to leave specific artworks to specific individuals, label each piece and its intended recipient using your inventory details. Add contingency instructions in case a work is unavailable or circumstances change. The clearer your direction, the easier it will be for your executor to carry out your wishes.

> Remember that receiving artwork is both a gift and a responsibility. It may require space, care, insurance, storage, and future decisions. It can also carry deep emotion. Not everyone is ready—or able—to take that on, even if they love you.

It can be generous to ask in advance which artworks—of those you consider available—someone would truly cherish. This is especially meaningful with children. Instead of assigning pieces, consider inviting heirs into the process. Walk the studio together. Give them sticky-notes or colored stickers. Share the stories of your artworks. Alternatively, you can allow them to select favorites through your artwork inventory system.

Giving people the opportunity to choose can transform the experience. It reduces misunderstanding, honors their autonomy, and helps the eventual distribution feel thoughtful and loving rather than imposed.

In your executor instructions, you might note that certain works were pre-selected by family members, reference where those preferences are documented, and authorize your executor to honor those selections before making any final distributions.

What to Include in Executor Instructions

Below is a list of items to include in the instructions for your executor. If you've completed the previous steps, most of what you need is already in (or referenced by) the **ART ESTATE NAVIGATOR.** If you notice gaps, return to those earlier steps and fill them in. As you review this list, you may find places where a bit more detail will help ensure your artwork and studio are handled according to your wishes.

1. Start with the Inventory — Describe the system you used to document your artwork, and whether the inventory is complete. Note that the inventory is the starting point for all decisions. Clarify categories, condition, estimated value (if known), income relevance, and intent notes. Indicate whether conservation is needed, especially for your owned art.

2. Define Finances and Income Streams — Identify galleries, consignment relationships, licensing agreements, royalties, editions, commissions, grants, and any recurring revenue sources. Clarify which arrangements should continue, be evaluated, renegotiated, or wound down. Document account information related to the business practice, including dedicated bank accounts, credit cards, payment processors, online sales platforms, bookkeeping systems, tax records, inventory tracking software, and outstanding invoices or receivables. Note subscription services, storage fees, insurance policies, and any automatic payments tied to the studio. Clear documentation prevents accidental termination of income, missed payments, or unnecessary financial loss during transition.

3. Protect Provenance — Preserve certificates of authenticity, exhibition records, sales history, installation notes, artist statements, and archives. Keep documentation connected to the work whenever possible.

4. Gifts and Donations — Name intended organization and individual recipients. State how firm the instruction is. Indicate whether substitutions or redirection are allowed.

5. Identify What Should Not Be Sold — Clearly list protected works, intact bodies of work, destruction directives, or required consultation before sale.

6. Provide Sales Guidance — Offer direction for gallery-represented work, higher-value works, and when professional consultation is required.

7. Authorize Use of Advisors — Encourage consultation when complexity, value, or uncertainty warrants it.

8. Grant Permission to Discard — Authorize disposal of hazardous, duplicative, or non-inventory materials while protecting listed works, income-producing assets, and archives.

CONFIRM LEGAL INTEGRATION

If this planning process has clarified or changed your intentions, make sure those changes are reflected in your legally binding estate documents.

Planning and legal authority should align.

Clarity creates freedom for you today, and for others tomorrow.

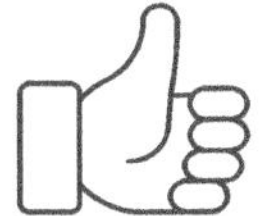

GOOD ENOUGH GUIDANCE
Thoughtful stewardship of your estate matters more than perfection, when developing your instructions.

Keep this in mind:
- Authority comes first.
- Stabilize and protect next.
- Use the inventory as the guide.
- Review finances before making decisions.
- Documentation protects value.
- Professional advice reduces risk.

COMPASS CHECK-IN

Take a breath. You've done meaningful work here.

As you look across your entire art estate—and by now you know what that includes—ask yourself: what do you truly want for it? What could you still do today to strengthen it?

Sometimes the act of organizing sparks new energy: a fresh body of work, a technique you've been meaning to try, a gallery you're finally ready to approach. Yes, writing instructions for after you're gone can feel heavy, especially when age taps you on the shoulder. But unless you've been given an expiration date, this isn't about winding down. It's about resetting your studio for what comes next. As Satchel Paige asked, *"How old would you be if you didn't know your age?"*

Now, gently pressure-test what you've written:

- If something happened tomorrow, would my executor feel guided—or guessing?
- Are my values and priorities easy to see?
- Have I made the decisions only I can make?
- Does my executor know where this information lives?
- Have I told them?

Clarity creates freedom for you today, and for others tomorrow.

REMINDER: ART ESTATE NAVIGATOR

Bring the **ART ESTATE NAVIGATOR** up to date by referencing the location of your Executor Instructions.

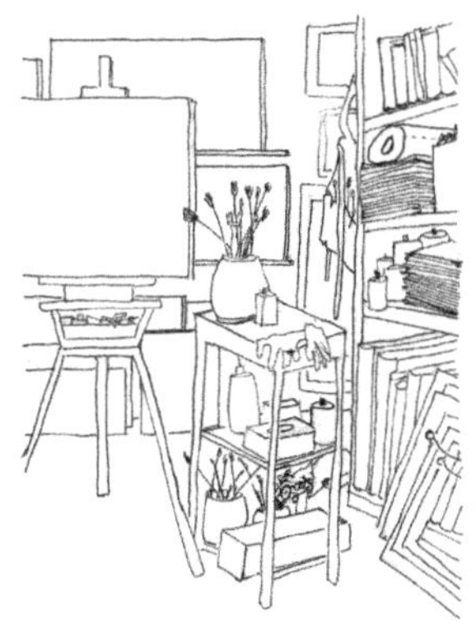

STEP 9: COMPLETE DOWNSIZING, & DISBURSEMENT OF A STUDIO

WHY THIS STEP MATTERS

Reaching this point marks a meaningful threshold. For artists, reaching this step often brings mixed emotions. Seeing artwork set aside, destroyed, or released can feel like a reckoning—not only with objects, but with time, effort, ambition, and identity. That response is normal. Finishing this work does not diminish the art that mattered, traveled, or endured. It acknowledges that not every piece needs to be carried forward for the legacy to remain intact.

For artists, completing this project means it is finished in principle. Everything has been reviewed, decisions have been made, and nothing essential remains unresolved. What continues—if anything—does so by choice, not by accumulation or avoidance.

> For many artists, reaching this point of completion feels less like an ending and more like the beginning of a new body of work.

For executors, completion looks slightly different. The work of assessment, sorting, and disposition may be complete, but stewardship can continue if the estate includes ongoing value. This may involve maintaining websites, managing archives, responding to inquiries, or overseeing the business aspects of the artist's work after death. These are not signs that the project failed to conclude; they are extensions built on a solid foundation.

What matters most is that the hard work has been done. The inventory is clear. The decisions are documented. The estate is intelligible to others. Whether the next phase involves quiet closure or continued activity, it rests on clarity rather than burden.

When artists don't leave guidance, their work often survives by accident—or disappears through confusion. When artists do leave guidance, something remarkable happens: the work carries context. It carries intention. It continues to communicate even when the artist is no longer present to explain it.

You did not accumulate the art and materials overnight. You spent years—maybe decades—looking longer than most people look, noticing what others passed by, and returning to the same questions: What matters? What do I see? What is worth saying, even if it takes a lifetime to say it?

This is legacy—not as a monument, but as continuity.

Art is not just what remains on the wall or in the studio. It is the accumulated result of attention, persistence, doubt, revision, and care. It is how you organized your understanding of the world—and then offered that understanding back to it.

By taking on this work of planning, organizing, and clarifying what happens next, you are not stepping away from your art. You are extending it.

This process is not about control. It is about care. Care for the work you made, for the people who will one day stand in the middle of your studio and wonder what to do, and for the life embedded in the objects you leave behind.

Your art reflects how you saw the world. It reveals what you valued, what you resisted, what you loved enough to wrestle with repeatedly. For your family and for future viewers, this clarity is a gift. It helps them understand not only what you made, but who you were.

Taking on this task is an act of generosity. It says: I care how this story continues.

And that is a final, meaningful work.

NOTE TO EXECUTORS

You have been entrusted with something that is both practical and profound.

Yes, there is work to be done, inventory to review, decisions to make, timelines and logistics to manage. But there is also something quieter unfolding beneath the tasks: the chance to carry forward a life's way of seeing.

As you move through this process, you are not expected to become an art expert. You are asked to become a steward—someone who acts thoughtfully, efficiently, and in good faith, using the tools and guidance that have been left for you.

This work can be done well without being overwhelming. Clear instructions, professional advisors, and a structured approach make it manageable. And when handled with care, it offers tangible benefits: financial value for heirs, reduced confusion and conflict, and decisions that honor both practicality and intention.

But beyond efficiency, there is meaning here.

Through this process, families often come to understand the artist in

> An artist's work is not simply a collection of objects. It is evidence of time spent paying attention. Of choosing to interpret rather than ignore. Of offering a perspective shaped by patience, discipline, personal philosophy, teachers, critiques, and imagination.

their midst more fully—why the work mattered, how it developed, what it was trying to say. The art becomes a bridge across generations, a way of keeping the artist present not just in memory, but in conversation.

By handling this responsibility with care and respect, you help ensure that the artist's work continues to speak—to collectors, to institutions, to family members, and to the wider world. You help extend the life of the work they labored to create.

IN THE END, THE ART

Six days prior to my friend Veronica's death, I sat in her living room overlooking Lake Michigan. She was in her hospital bed, her caregiver sat quietly engaged in a book, a few feet away. Veronica asked me to retrieve a manila folder holding pastel paintings from a file drawer in her bedroom. My visit lasted much longer than I expected as we went through the rather slim, curated selection of her art. Heart failure left her with little breath and little energy, until... We began talking about art.

I held up a painting of a sharply cut mountainous shoreline in Hawaii. She smiled as she remembered that her husband Matt had been standing beside her when she took the photo. She described the short, curving strokes she used to create movement in the clouds, and the blues, greens, reds and yellows that churned the waves. Ronnie asked me to flip the paper over so we could read her notes on the back. They described the warmth of the sun and the fragrance in the winds that inspired her scene.

Later, I was told ours was the last full conversation of her life.

Two years earlier, after Matt died and she moved into independent living, she gave away several paintings and supplies to friends. I filled my car with papers, frames, mats, an easel, and other equipment pulled from closets and drawers and delivered them to the Waste Shed, an art recycling center. With her encouragement, I kept a couple of sketchbooks. What remained was a single drawer: a thin folder of small pastel paintings, two sketchbooks, paper, pencils, and one box of favorite pastels.

At her memorial service, the paintings from that folder were displayed beside photos of her travels with Matt. Her family gifted me the Hawaiian shoreline — though I hardly needed an object to remember her.

When you know an artist is actively dying, show them their work. Talk about it. It is their life. It gives you something real to hold onto together. You may learn one new thing. You may give them the comfort of knowing their work mattered.

And if you are an artist, know this: you do not stop being an artist. Even if months — or years — have passed since you last picked up a chisel, brush, or pencil, your art is still there.

Keep a photo book of your favorite creations nearby. When things go quiet, pull it out and ask, "Would you like to see what I've been working on?"

-----END-----

ACKNOWLEDGMENTS

Before closing, I want to acknowledge the many people who helped shape this project. To ensure the information is accurate and the tone grounded in real experience, I spoke with professional and emerging artists, as well as dedicated hobbyists—many of them standing in studios full of decades of accumulation, wondering what comes next. I learned from gallerists who represent older artists, from artists who have thoughtfully cleared their studios and discovered not only fewer obstacles underfoot but renewed energy for new work. I sought attorney review, listened carefully to the next generation—who may or may not want as much art as we imagine—and even spoke with an art recycling center to understand responsible alternatives. My sincere thanks to all of you for your candor, wisdom, and generosity: Claire Conley, Mary Gingrich, Errol Jacobson, Kendra Kett, William Marvin, Karen Menighen, Elizabeth Murphy, Kimberly Oliva, Beth Peterson, Steve Puttrich, Daria Shvets, Nick Sistler, Lee Solock, Kathryn Somers, and Stephanie Weidner.

And most especially, my deepest gratitude to my family—
Alex Frederick, Jim Longe and Karen Longe for their patience, their honest conversations, editing, and their steady encouragement as this work took shape.

ABOUT THE AUTHOR

Mary Longe holds a certificate in Art Business from Sotheby's Institute of Art, London. She lectures on Navigating the Art Marketplace for Emerging Artists and Collectors, and lectures and provides coaching on the Art Legacy Compass. Longe is a mom, and the former executive director of Plein Air Painters Chicago. She is also an artist, who paints and creates multimedia artworks with an eye on the current socio-political experience. Longe's collage art has been critiqued in Made in Bed Magazine, and her plein air art in New City online magazine. Besides her art and writing life, Mary Longe's professional career included twenty years working for the American Hospital Association, and seventeen years, as founder and CEO of Longe Life Libraries, which designed specialty consumer health libraries for health care organizations and other businesses. She can be reached at artlegacy-compass@gmail.com.

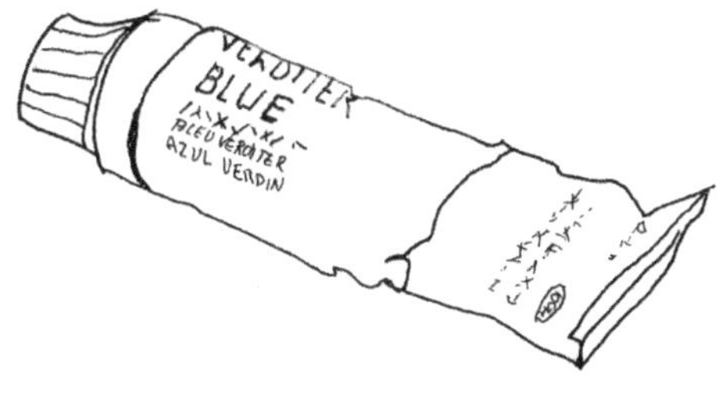

APPENDIX

The Appendix contains three working sections: the Artist Packet, the Executor Packet, and Additional Resources. Together, they translate the nine-step process in this book into organized, practical documentation.

The **ARTIST PACKET** is meant to be completed while you are living. As you move through each of the nine steps, fill in the corresponding sections of the **ART ESTATE NAVIGATOR** and supporting worksheets. These pages capture your decisions and become the working foundation of your art estate plan. Use the checklists as guides, and download editable versions at www.artlegacycompass.com if that makes the process easier.

The **EXECUTOR PACKET** is for the person who will one day carry out your instructions. Once you have clarified your decisions, take time to personalize these materials so they clearly reflect your intent. This packet offers steady guidance during what can be a complex and transitional period.

APPENDIX – ARTIST PACKET

- **ART ESTATE NAVIGATOR**
- **CHECKLIST – FOR MY EXECUTOR – FIRST 90 DAYS**
- **MEETING WITH ATTORNEY – DISCUSSION GUIDE**
- **DISPOSITION INSTRUCTIONS**
- **PARAGRAPHS – AUTHORITY FOR ART ESTATE AND ADMINISTRATION**
- **EMAIL COVER TO ATTORNEY – ART DISPOSITION AND COPYRIGHT**

APPENDIX – EXECUTOR PACKET

- **EXECUTOR'S ART ESTATE ADMINISTRATION GUIDE**
- **NOTIFICATION OF DEATH**
- **STORAGE, INSURANCE AND CONDITION PROTECTION PROTOCOL**

ADDITIONAL RESOURCES

- **JOB DESCRIPTION – INVENTORY CATALOGER**
- **CLEARING A STUDIO – 15 KEY POINTS ABOUT THRIFT, CONSIGNMENT AND RESALE OUTLETS**
- **VETTING CHECKLIST – ART DEALERS, ADVISORS AND AGENTS**

DOWNLOAD CUSTOMIZABLE WORKSHEETS AND UP-TO-DATE LISTS AT WWW.ARTLEGACYCOMPASS.COM

ART LEGACY PROJECT — PROGRESS TRACKER

☐ Yes — Date: ___________ Project Defined

☐ Yes — Date: ___________ Income Streams Identified

☐ Yes — Date: ___________ For My Executor — First 90 Days Completed

☐ Yes — Date: ___________ Inventory Completed

☐ Yes — Date: ___________ ART ESTATE NAVIGATOR Completed

☐ Yes — Date: ___________ Disposition Instructions Listed

☐ Yes — Date: ___________ Executor Packet Assembled

☐ Yes — Date: ___________ Will or Trust Updated

APPENDIX | STEP 1 ART ESTATE NAVIGATOR - UPDATE THROUGHOUT THE PROJECT

This worksheet is a personal planning tool to help you describe your art business to an executor or trustee. While it's not a legal document, it organizes key details that will form the basis of your Executor Instructions. Though not a standalone legal instrument, it should be shared with your attorney. Account numbers, passwords and other personal data should be secured separately.

SECTION 1 – ARTIST AND BUSINESS IDENTIFICATION

Legal Name: ____

Professional Name (if different): ___________________________________

Business Name (if any): ____

Business Structure: ☐ Sole Proprietorship ☐ LLC ☐ Corporation
☐ Partnership ☐ Unsure

State Formed (if different than current address): _____________________

Federal EIN (if applicable): _______________________________________

Primary Studio Address: ____

Additional Studio or Storage Locations: ____________________________

SECTION 2 – WHAT CONSTITUTES MY ART ESTATE

To provide an overview of your art estate, begin by checking the boxes that describe its elements. As you continue to organize, come back to this section to include more details, such as general descriptions, quantities.

☐ Finished artworks (list media)

☐ Works in progress

☐ Studies, sketches, maquettes, proofs

☐ Editions (sold / unsold)

☐ Digital works and files

☐ NFTs and blockchain-based works

☐ Archives (photographs, slides, negatives, notebooks, correspondence)

☐ Tools, presses, molds, equipment, plates, and materials

☐ Copyrights and intellectual property

☐ Leases, studio properties, vehicles, other art-related assets

☐ Art-related business records

☐ Art you own by other artists

☐ Other

SECTION 3 – LOCATIONS OF ART ESTATE ITEMS

List all the places where items in your art estate might be found.

☐ Primary locations: (Workspace, home, garage, attic, basement, specific drawers, etc.)

☐ Items on loan:____

☐ Works on consignment:____

☐ Storage units: ____

☐ Access instructions: (Location and keys/passcodes) _________________

____

SECTION 4 – ONGOING INCOME STREAMS

List all sources of income, Note for each: 1) Description of income; 2) Location of contracts, invoices, correspondence; 3) Tax forms (1099s) expected; 4) Key Contacts; 5) Passwords (or their location); 6) For online sources include log in credentials; 7) Status: active, occasional, discontinued.

☐ Gallery-based income

☐ Print-on-demand or digital sales

☐ Royalties and licensing agreements

☐ Teaching income

☐ Books, teaching materials, recordings

☐ Outstanding Commissions

☐ Instructions regarding continuation or closure: ____________________

SECTION 5 – BUSINESS AND FINANCIAL MATTERS

☐ Bank Accounts (types & institution only): ________________________

☐ Financial Services Platforms (PayPal, Zelle, Venmo): _______________

☐ Receivables owed to artist (list location): _______________________

☐ Outstanding debts or obligations: ______________________________

☐ Insurance carrier and policy location:___________________________

Professional Assistance (accountant, bookkeeper, financial planner):

____

☐ Transit or exhibition insurance instructions:_____________________

SECTION 6 – EXECUTOR AND PROFESSIONAL CONTACTS

Ensure the right people have the right authority.

☐ Primary Executor: ____

☐ Art Advisor / Art Executor: ____________________________________

☐ Estate Attorney: ____

☐ Insurance Agent: ____

☐ Other professionals to contact: ________________________________

SECTION 7 – COPYRIGHT AND INTELLECTUAL PROPERTY

(Discuss meaning and appropriate use with an attorney.)

Physical artwork and copyright are separate assets.

Copyright holder(s):____

Registration status: ____

Reproduction instructions: _____________________________________

Moral rights preferences:_______________________________________

SECTION 8 – GALLERY RELATIONSHIPS AND CONSIGNMENTS

Current galleries: ____

Past galleries with representation: _______________________________

Exclusive or non-exclusive agreements: ___________________________

SECTION 9 – PROVENANCE AND AUTHENTICATION (OWNED ART)

Location of receipts and documentation: _______________________________

Conservation or restoration records: _________________________________

SECTION 10 – PROVENANCE AND AUTHENTICATION (ARTIST'S WORK)

Location of biography, exhibition history, awards: _______________________

Location of sales records: ____

Authority to authenticate works posthumously. ☐ Yes ☐ No

Procedures for disputed works: _______________________________________

SECTION 11 – DISPOSITION INTENTIONS (WITH NOTES OR LINK TO INVENTORY)

☐ Works to be sold ____

☐ Works to be gifted ____

☐ Works to be donated____

☐ Works to be retained by heirs ______________________________________

☐ Works to be destroyed or recycled __________________________________

☐ Priority order or special notes:_____________________________________

SECTION 12 – STUDIO AND STORAGE TRANSITION / FOUNDRY OR OTHER PROCESSING

Names: ____

Locations:____

Access instructions:____

Vacate timeline (if applicable): ______________________________________

Insurance instructions during transition: ______________________________

Transport plan: ____

SECTION 13 – DIGITAL ASSETS

Website / domain ownership: ____

Social media accounts: ____

NFT's location and related wallets: _______________________________________

Cloud storage locations: ____

Other digital subscriptions (professional or marketing): _________________

Secure password protocol location (not passwords):______________________

SECTION 14 – LEGACY AND INSTITUTIONAL INTENTIONS

Institutions to notify (include contact name):_________________________

Archive or study collection aspirations:_______________________________

Restrictions on sale of specific bodies of work:_______________________

SECTION 15 – HIGH-VALUE OR SENSITIVE ITEMS

Works requiring professional handling: _______________________________

Items to be returned: ____

Authorization regarding destruction of unsellable works:________________

APPENDIX | STEP 1 – ART ESTATE NAVIGATOR ADDITIONS AND REVISIONS

After each addition or revision in the document, use the signature page to note your progress—this keeps you on track as you move forward.

Artist Name: ____

Date of Original Version:_____________________________________

Locations of Current Signed Version of ART ESTATE NAVIGATOR

Physical location: ____

Digital location: ____

Initial Acknowledgment

Signature: ________________________________   Date: ___________

Revision History

Description of Update: _________________   Initials: ______ Date: __________

Description of Update: _________________   Initials: ______ Date: __________

Description of Update: _________________   Initials: ______ Date: __________

Description of Update: _________________   Initials: ______ Date: __________

Description of Update: _________________   Initials: ______ Date: __________

Description of Update: _________________   Initials: ______ Date: __________

APPENDIX | STEP 1 – ARTIST PACKET

CHECKLIST – FOR MY EXECUTOR - FIRST 90 DAYS

This document provides a concise overview to orient you to the art estate and outlines immediate steps to protect it before major decisions are made.

Data from the **ART ESTATE NAVIGATOR** will apply to this much briefer checklist.

Executor Checklist – If I'm Gone Tomorrow – First 90 Days

Purpose: Orientation and protection before decisions are made.

FIRST 0–30 DAYS

- Contact Attorney:
- Secure studios and storage
- Locate digital and hard copy files, and other estate documents
- Confirm executor authority
- Notify attorney and insurers
- Open estate bank account you will need an appropriate EIN from the IRS
- Pause all sales, donations, disposal, and licensing

31–90 DAYS

- Redirect income streams
- Track income and expenses
- Review inventory and income sources
- Confirm what can and cannot move legally

REMINDERS

- Do not assume ownership
- No commingling of funds
- Income continuity may be critical
- Consult professionals when uncertain

APPENDIX | STEP 1 – ARTIST PACKET

MEETING WITH ATTORNEY – DISCUSSION GUIDE

This list is designed to help you prepare for informed conversations with your attorney or estate planner. It is not legal advice, but a planning tool to help ensure that your artwork and related assets are addressed clearly and intentionally. The STEPs listed indicate where these topics are discussed in the Guide.

Visual artwork is unlike most other properties. It may function simultaneously as tangible property, intellectual property, business inventory, and cultural record. The following sections help you think through what should be discussed and clarified in your estate documents.

The following can be derived from the information collected in the **ART ESTATE NAVIGATOR:**

1. Artist and Business Identification
2. What Makes Up the Art Estate
3. Where Things Are
4. Ongoing Income Streams
5. Business and Financial Matters
6. Executors and Professionals
7. Copyright and Intellectual Property
8. Galleries and Consignments
9. Provenance (Owned Art)
10. Provenance (Artist's Work)
11. Disposition Intentions
12. Studio and Storage Transition
13. Digital Assets
14. Legacy and Institutional Intentions
15. High-Value or Sensitive Items

The following are additional items to consider

16. Authority Items - Confirm your representative may manage the practical realities of your art estate. Authority to:
    - Access studios, storage spaces, and archives
    - Enter contracts related to artwork administration
    - Negotiate pricing and terms
    - Sell, donate, gift, destroy works
    - Complete, sell, archive, destroy unfinished works
    - Hire art professionals
    - Continue or wind down art business
    - Indemnification for executor acting in good faith
    - Copyright transfer or licensing provisions
    - Delegate

17. Liquidity and Administration Costs - Consider and communicate how estate expenses will be covered so gifts do not require forced sales.
    - Funding for packing, shipping, insurance, appraisal, storage, conservation, and legal expenses
    - Authorization to use estate funds for art-related administration
    - Executor and advisor compensation
    - Works to be donated
    - Works to be retained by heirs
    - Works to be recycled or destroyed
    - Restrictions on sale of specific bodies of work

18. Optional Letter of Intent - Letter explaining values, priorities, and legacy intentions

APPENDIX STEP 8 – ARTIST PACKET

DISPOSITION INSTRUCTIONS

Disposition Overview

This section helps you document how your artwork and studio materials should be handled in the future. Your goal is to provide clear written instructions so your executor understands how each category of work should be placed. Use your inventory (or an attached list) to indicate which artworks may be sold, donated, gifted, specifically bequeathed, or discarded, depending on their value and significance. Be as specific as necessary to prevent confusion. Clear categorization now will make future decisions easier and more consistent with your intent.

Personal Bequests

If you wish to leave specific artworks to specific individuals, clearly identify each piece and its intended recipient using your inventory details. Consider including contingency instructions in case a work is unavailable or circumstances change. The clearer your direction, the easier it will be for your executor to carry out your wishes.

Additional sections address sales, charitable donations, and final disposal. Thoughtfully completing each category creates a comprehensive disposition plan and reduces uncertainty for those who will later implement it.

Disposition Cover for Executor

Dear Executor,

Thank you for honoring my wishes. This guide is your compass through the disposition of my work—whether selling, donating, gifting to individuals I've named. Each section provides clear steps so you can ensure every piece is handled as I intended. By following these instructions, you'll help carry forward my wishes with care and clarity.

APPENDIX | STEP 8 – ARTIST PACKET
PARAGRAPHS – AUTHORITY FOR ART ESTATE ADMINISTRATION
For Will – Executor, and Trust – Trustee

Executor Paragraph – Authority for Art Estate Administration

I grant my Executor full power and discretion to manage and administer my artwork and related materials, including all finished and unfinished works, studies, archives, tools, and associated intellectual property rights. My Executor may inventory, authenticate, photograph, appraise, insure, store, conserve, exhibit, loan, license, sell, donate, destroy, or otherwise dispose of such property, at such times and on such terms as my Executor determines appropriate, with or without court approval.

My Executor is authorized to retain and compensate qualified professionals as needed and shall not be liable for good-faith decisions made in reliance on my written art estate instructions, inventories, or related documentation.

Trustee Paragraph – Authority for Art Estate Administration

I grant my Trustee full power and discretion to administer my artwork and related materials as a distinct class of trust property, including all finished and unfinished works, studies, archives, tools, and associated intellectual property rights. The Trustee may inventory, authenticate, photograph, appraise, insure, store, conserve, exhibit, loan, license, sell, donate, destroy, or otherwise dispose of such property, at such times and on such terms as the Trustee determines appropriate.

The Trustee is authorized to retain and compensate qualified professionals as needed and shall not be liable for good-faith decisions made in reliance on my written art estate instructions, inventories, or related documentation.

APPENDIX | STEP 8 – ARTIST PACKET
EMAIL COVER TO ATTORNEY – ART DISPOSITION AND COPYRIGHT

To: ____

I am sharing a document titled "Art Disposition and Copyright Instructions for my Executor." This document is intended to operate alongside my will or trust and provides guidance on how authority is to be exercised for art assets.

Please confirm receipt and review for consistency with my estate documents, including authority, funding, discretion, and art-specific provisions.

Thank you,

[Your Name]

EXECUTOR PACKET

APPENDIX | STEP 8 – EXECUTOR PACKET

EXECUTOR'S ART ESTATE ADMINISTRATION GUIDE

This guide provides structured direction for administering an artist's estate.

It works alongside the Will or Trust and should be used together with the DISTRIBUTION INSTRUCTIONS, which reference the ART ESTATE NAVIGATOR, inventory, and related estate documents.

Its purpose is to help the executor:

- Exercise their authority thoughtfully and appropriately

- Protect artwork and related assets

- Follow the artist's documented intentions

- Make decisions in a clear and defensible order

This guide does not replace legal documents. It organizes and explains how to carry out the responsibilities those documents authorize.

Governing Principles

- Authority precedes action.

- Inventory precedes movement.

- Income streams require review before termination.

- Documentation remains with the work.

- Financial control must be established before disposition.

- Thoughtful reduction is part of stewardship.

Phased Administration Framework

Phase 1 – Immediate Stabilization: Secure physical and digital assets. Confirm authority. Preserve insurance coverage. Freeze irreversible actions.

Phase 2 – Authority and Financial Control: Establish legal and financial control. Redirect income. Clarify ownership and copyright. Prevent commingling.

Phase 3 – Organization and Informed Action: Verify inventory and documentation. Review provenance and contractual obligations. Begin instructed sales, gifts, donations, and disposal.

Phase 4 – Consolidation and Reduction: Finalize placements. Reduce storage. Resolve archives and digital presence. Wind down business operations as appropriate.

Phase 5 – Long-Term Stewardship (If Applicable): Monitor licensing, respond to institutional inquiries, and manage any ongoing rights or obligations as directed by estate documents.

Critical Action Checklist and Timeline

Immediate Actions (First 24–30 Days)

- Notify estate attorneys and confirm authority under Will or Trust. (See below)
- Obtain EIN and open an estate bank account.
- Secure studios, storage units, and digital assets. (See below)
- Confirm climate control and protect artworks from risk. (See below)
- Locate inventory, insurance policies, contracts, and provenance records.
- Notify insurers and confirm coverage remains active.
- Pause all sales, donations, disposal, and licensing.

Short Term (First Year)

- Redirect and track income streams.
- Avoid commingling of funds.
- Verify and update inventory.
- Review provenance and contractual obligations.
- Complete condition reports before movement.
- Begin instructed sales, gifts, and donations.
- Secure and manage digital presence.

Medium Term

- Complete placement and disposition.
- Reduce storage and administrative burden.
- Manage copyright and licensing.
- Wind down business operations as directed.

Long Term (If Applicable)

- Monitor licensing income.

- Respond to institutional inquiries.

- Close remaining accounts when obligations conclude.

APPENDIX | STEP 8 – EXECUTOR PACKET
NOTIFICATION OF DEATH

Subject: Notice of Death – [Artist's Name]

Hello [Organization/Gallery Name],

I am writing to notify you of the death of [Artist's Name].

I am the appointed executor. Please direct all inquiries regarding artwork, representation, consignments, or image use to:

[Executor Name]

[Email]

[Phone]

[Address]

Thank you.

Sincerely,

[Executor's Name]

APPENDIX | STEP 5 – EXECUTOR PACKET
STORAGE, INSURANCE, AND CONDITION PROTECTION PROTOCOL

Trigger Event: Upon notification of death, the executor should immediately determine what that event activates—authority under the Will or Trust, insurance notifications, access permissions, storage contracts, consignment agreements, or loan obligations. Document the date and time of death, as certain policies and contracts may have reporting requirements.

Immediate (First 24–72 Hours): Secure all studio and storage locations. Confirm environmental stability and protect artworks from physical risk. Limit unnecessary handling.

Within First Week: Notify the insurance carrier as required. Confirm policy validity, coverage limits, and any requirements related to transit, storage, or valuation.

Before Movement: Photograph works in place and complete condition documentation before any relocation or consolidation.

Ongoing: Maintain climate-controlled storage where appropriate, document any damage, and keep digital copies of inventories, policies, and key documents securely stored and backed up.

ADDITIONAL APPENDIX

APPENDIX | STEP 3

JOB DESCRIPTION – ARTWORK INVENTORY CATALOGER

If the inventory is large in volume or size, you may want assistance. Use the following template to post a position for assistance to inventory artwork. Include any specific information to fit your situation.

ART INVENTORY & CATALOGING (PART-TIME)

Position Overview

Part-time position responsible for documenting, organizing, and maintaining a structured inventory of artworks created by the artist and works owned by the artist using an app-based or Excel system. Supports professional record-keeping, studio organization, and future planning.

Responsibilities

- Maintain inventory for approximately X artworks.
- Assign and track accession numbers.
- Photograph artworks (front, back, details).
- Upload images and enter core data (title, medium, dimensions, date, status, location, notes).
- Match provenance materials for owned works; assist with basic valuation research.
- Maintain organized digital and physical records.
- Support collector-facing social media (Instagram, Facebook, TikTok).

Schedule [ ] hours per week.

Qualifications

- Strong organizational and data entry skills
- Proficiency in Microsoft Word and Excel
- Attention to detail and ability to work independently
- Careful handling of artwork

Preferred

- Knowledge of contemporary and modern visual art
- Familiarity with art markets, collections, or valuation
- Experience with inventory or digital asset systems
- Familiarity with Social Media

Education

Backgrounds in Art Business, Art History, Gallery or Museum Management, Collections, or equivalent experience.

Keywords for use with social media: Art Inventory; Art Cataloging; Cataloger; Collections Management; Curator; Provenance; Artwork Documentation; Studio Management; Digital Asset Management

APPENDIX | STEP 7

CLEARING A STUDIO – 15 KEY POINTS ABOUT THRIFT, CONSIGNMENT AND RESALE OUTLETS

Here's a practical guide for artists and executors managing the disposition of artwork, supplies, equipment, and furniture.

1. **National Thrift Chains (Goodwill, Salvation Army)**

   Pros: Easy drop-off, broad acceptance, potential tax-deductible donation

   Cons: No direct payment; limited control over pricing or placement

2. **Faith-Based Thrift Stores (St. Vincent de Paul)**

   Pros: Community-centered mission; often accept furniture and household goods

   Cons: Donation-based; resale value not returned to donor

3. **Regional Thrift Stores**

   Pros: Less restrictive intake; useful for various studio contents

   Cons: Lower resale values; limited specialization

4. **Community Resale Shops**

   Pros: Local impact; mission-driven organizations

   Cons: Selective intake; smaller scale operations

5. **Consignment Shops**

   Pros: Potential income; curated presentation of items

   Cons: Selective acceptance; sales may take time

6. **High-End / Luxury Consignment**

   Pros: Best for high-quality furniture, décor, or notable items

   Cons: Strict standards; limited intake

7. **Furniture-Focused Resale Shops**

   Pros: Ideal for easels, shelving, stools, and storage units

   Cons: Condition, size, and style matter

8. **Vintage & Salvage Warehouses**

   Pros: Good outlet for industrial furniture, frames, racks, shelving

   Cons: Not suitable for small or low-value items

9. Creative Reuse Centers

Pros: Excellent for art supplies, materials, and tools

Cons: Donation-based; no direct compensation

10. Specialty Art-Adjacent Resale

Pros: May understand studio equipment and art-related materials

Cons: Limited scope; inconsistent intake policies

11. Online Local Resale (Facebook Marketplace, Craigslist)

Pros: Direct income; local buyers; flexible pricing

Cons: Time-intensive; requires coordination and communication

12. Online Marketplaces (eBay, Etsy)

Pros: Broad reach; good for niche or specialized items

Cons: Listing effort, fees, shipping logistics

13. Estate & Downsizing Services

Pros: Comprehensive clearing; minimal effort required

Cons: Service fees; less control over outcomes

14. Donation for Tax Benefit

Pros: Documentation may offset income taxes

Cons: Appraisal required for higher-value items

15. Partial Liquidation Strategy

Pros: Maximizes value by matching items to the best outlet

Cons: Requires planning, coordination, and tracking

APPENDIX | STEP 7

VETTING CHECKLIST: DEALERS, ADVISORS AND AGENTS

Before engaging any professional, clarify roles, incentives, and expectations. For established artists, even small transactions can affect long-term value.

Core questions for any professional:

- What role are you playing—seller, broker, advisor, or coordinator?
- How are you compensated, and by whom?
- Do you have financial relationships with recommended outlets?
- How do you manage conflicts of interest?

Additional Questions for Art Dealers

- Have you sold comparable work by this artist or similar artists?
- Where do you expect the work to go?
- How is pricing determined, and will results be public or private?
- Is there a written agreement covering insurance, timing, and payment?

Red flags:

Vague resale plans, pressure to move volume quickly, or reluctance to put terms in writing.

Additional Questions for Advisors and Agents

- Are you advising or negotiating on my behalf?
- Do you receive referral fees, and are they disclosed?
- How will you sequence sales across galleries, dealers, auctions, or platforms?
- How will progress and outcomes be reported?

Executor Safeguards

- Do not rush decisions without documentation
- Avoid exclusivity unless time-bound and clearly beneficial
- Keep written records of all terms and communications
- When uncertain, pause—market opportunities are rarely one-time events

Final Reminder

Good professionals bring clarity, not urgency. For established artists especially, the right dealer or advisor acts less like a salesperson and more like a steward—helping match work to the right audience while protecting both value and reputation.

NOTES